Part 1
Ground Zero

Moving from
Shattered to Strong

THE FOUNDATIONS OF RECOVERY

From Sexual Addiction And Intimacy Avoidance

Matt Burton
Kevin Rose
Laura Burton

Part 1
Ground Zero

Moving from
Shattered to Strong

THE FOUNDATIONS OF RECOVERY

From Sexual Addiction
And Intimacy Avoidance

MATT BURTON
KEVIN ROSE
LAURA BURTON

Part 1
Ground Zero

Moving from
Shattered to Strong

THE
FOUNDATIONS
OF RECOVERY

From Sexual Addiction
And Intimacy Avoidance

MATT BURTON
KEVIN ROSE
LAURA BURTON

Copyright © 2025 by Becoming Well, LLC

All rights reserved. No part of this book may be reproduced or transmitted in any form, or by any means, electronic or mechanical, including photocopying, recording, or by information storage or retrieval systems, without permission in writing from the copyright owner.

The views and opinions expressed in this book are those of the author and do not necessarily reflect the official policy or position of Becoming Well, LLC

Published by Becoming Well, LLC

www.BecomingWellInstitute.com

Library of Congress Control Number

Paperback ISBN: 979-8-3493-4150-2

E-book ISBN: 979-8-3493-8506-3

Cover design by Monira

Printed in the United States of America

Table of Contents

Recovery Tool Box 3

1. Exercise Book Completed in a Year 5
2. 3 Goals for Individuals, 3 couple goals for the next 52 weeks 6
3. Meetings 7
4. Phone Calls 8
5. 90 in 90 9
6. Choose a Sponsor 10
7. 30-Day Checklist 11
8. Weekly Check-In 12
9. 24-Hour Tell Policy 14
10. 100% Responsible 15
11. Rubber Band 16
12. Blockers and Accountability Software 18
13. Book Work 19
14. HALT BS 21
15. Gratitude List 23
16. Bookending 25

12 Steps in a Year 27

17. Step 1 29
18. Step 2 31
19. Step 3 33
20. Step 4 35
21. Step 5 37
22. Step 6 39
23. Step 7 41
24. Step 8 43
25. Step 9 45
26. Step 10 47
27. Step 11 49
28. Step 12 51

Helping My Partner Heal (Part 1) — 53

29. Rebuilding Trust Pyramid – Honesty — 55
30. Rebuilding Trust Pyramid – Safety — 57
31. Rebuilding Trust Pyramid – Consistency — 59
32. Rebuilding Trust Pyramid – Intimacy — 61
33. Standing Shoulder to Shoulder — 62
34. Demeanor - Part 1 — 65
35. 70/30 to 80/20 — 67
36. Stabilization — 68
37. Emptying the Pain Closet — 71
38. Empathy Exercise - (Hearing and validating) — 73
39. No Defend or Explain for the 13-Weeks Challenge — 77
40. Daily Check-In (ours): Daily, FANOS, Safer Check-In — 79
41. Feeling Wheel - You gotta feel it to heal it — 82
42. Most Flawed Moment — 84

Maintain a Sobriety Focus — 87

43. Staying Sober Checklist — 89
44. 3 Circles — 91
45. SA/PA Lapse and Relapse Worksheet — 93
46. Appreciation and Resignation Letters for SA/PA/Infidelity — 95
47. SA/PA Relapse Chain — 99
48. SA/PA Relapse Prevention Plan — 101
49. Top 5 Intimacy Avoidance — 103
50. Intimacy Avoidance – Appreciation and Resignation Letters — 105
51. IA Relapse Chain — 117
52. IA Relapse Prevention Plan — 118

Addendum — 121

40 ways to be IA (Intimacy Avoidant) — 129

Workgroups and Intensives — 135

Books and Courses — 143

AUTHORS' NOTE

Although the publisher and the authors have made every effort to ensure that the information in this book was correct at press time, and while this publication is designed to provide accurate information regarding the subject matter covered, the publisher and the authors assume no responsibility for errors, inaccuracies, omissions, or any other inconsistencies herein and hereby disclaim any liability to any party for any loss, damage, or disruption caused by errors or omissions, whether such errors or omissions result from negligence, accident, or any other cause.

This publication is meant as a source of valuable information for the reader. However, it is not meant as a substitute for direct expert assistance. If such a level of assistance is required, the services of a competent professional should be sought.

MATT AND LAURA BURTON
www.BecomingWellInstitute.com

INTRODUCTION

Welcome to Foundations of Recovery. Regardless of where you're at on your recovery journey, this workbook will help you chart a path of health. It will also benefit those hurt by your destructive behaviors and the ways of thinking connected to them. In short, *Foundations of Recovery* will help you get better.

This workbook was birthed out of 30-plus years of personal recovery and walking with thousands of men through their recovery journeys. Whether you are working on *Foundations of Recovery – Part 1: Ground Zero*, or *Foundations of Recovery – Part 2: Digging Deeper*, you will find that the exercises in this workbook will expand the depth of your recovery. It will also provide you with many, many tools to help you navigate and succeed in your individual and relational recovery.

Foundations of Recovery – Part 1: Ground Zero focuses on expanding your recovery toolbox, getting through the 12 steps in a year, and doing exercises around helping your partner heal, as well as maintaining a sobriety focus.

Foundations of Recovery – Part 2: Digging Deeper focuses on whether you are "all in" with regards to recovery, how to understand the destructiveness of lying and exercises to combat it, how objectification is so destructive, and how to change object thinking. It also offers a focus on helping your partner heal. You will be educated on the warning signs of potential relapse and given the tools you need to journey long-term through the marathon that is recovery.

Each workbook contains 52 exercises. We hope you will complete at least one exercise per week and finish this workbook in one year. For those wishing to accelerate their recovery, you will complete two exercises per week: one in *Foundations of Recovery – Part 1: Ground Zero*, and one in *Foundations of Recovery – Part 2: Digging Deeper*. Do this and you'll complete both workbooks in a year. Whether you get them done in one or two years, these workbooks, when done weekly and shared with your partner, will help you profoundly in your individual and relational recovery journey.

Other materials available through Becoming Well, LLC and our Becoming Well Institute here in Tucson, AZ may be helpful in your journey. They are listed in the appendix of this book with a full list on our website. Virtual sessions for individuals and couples, Recovery Workgroups, Couples Private Intensives, Couples Group Intensives, Wounded Partner Healing Intensives, Men's Recovery Intensives, and Men's Going Deeper Healing Intensives, as well as courses, books, and videos are also available worldwide.

Please contact us for further information.

You can visit our website at

www.BecomingWellInstitute.com

for access other resources for you and your partner

Becoming Well, LLC and Becoming Well Institute

Phone number: 520-355-5322

Email address: Info@MyBecomingWell.com

Recovery Tool Box

Exercise Book

Exercise 1

Completed in a Year

Between the two exercise books (*Foundations of Recovery – Part 1: Ground Zero* and *Part 2: Digging Deeper*), you will have 104 total exercises to complete over the next two years. Doing the math, this means 1 exercise per week. Pairing this expectation with the **Daily Times for Recovery**, you will be on track to complete them all. *Be aware that if you're in a Becoming Well Workgroup, you will have planned exercises (homework) to complete and discuss while in group 2-3 times monthly. This counts towards your expectation of 1 exercise per week.

Why do you have this expectation for yourself? Part of your growth in recovery, whether you are in a relationship or not, is creating habits of daily recovery for the rest of your life. Like your physical body, your heart and spirit need exercise to remain healthy. If you don't stay in recovery, you will drift out of health.

Think of a healthy habit you have developed in your life. How has it benefited you?

If you haven't kept up with the habit listed above, what did you begin to lose?

If you are ready to commit to this practice, this is great news! Share it with a recovery partner in a workgroup and a sponsor. I, _____(name), say _____(yes/no), I will commit to completing one exercise per week during my **Daily Times for Recovery**.

Steps 1-3 Connection: When we come together to recover, we do so with the power of accountability.

Share your commitment with another person.

How does it feel to be in community with others who are also seeking health?

On a recovery call, ask someone what this commitment has produced for them. Record their answer here.

PARTNER CONNECT Share your commitment to complete the 52 exercises with your partner. Who are you going to choose as an accountability partner to help hold you to this commitment?

 **Exercise 2**   **3 Goals**

If you don't have a goal, you're not going to reach it. In individual recovery and relational recovery, it's vital to make sure that you have goals that you both write out and periodically check to make sure that you are executing them well.

That's where 3 & 3 come in:
- 3 individual recovery goals
- 3 relationship recovery goals.

These are 12-month goals. You're going to write out three individual recovery goals.
Make these for yourself, for your SA recovery, and for your IA recovery.

1.
2.
3.

Next, you're going to write out relationship recovery goals. Again, do these independent of your partner. Make it come from your heart and your desires for your partnership.

1.
2.
3.

Share your relational goals with your partner. In these beginning stages of recovery, whatever their feelings may be about your goals, practice the **Empathy Exercise** regarding their feelings. Reflect here on your partner's feelings and how they are understandable in this stage of recovery.

Feeling:_____ Why it's understandable:

Feeling:_____ Why it's understandable:

Step 1 Connection: The powerlessness of this step is also designed to have you reflect on what *is* in your power. In a calendar one year from now, whether digitally in your device or on a hardcopy calendar, set a reminder to reflect on your 3 & 3.

<u>**PARTNER CONNECT**</u> Share your goals with your partner.

Meetings

Exercise 3

Do you remember the feeling you had when you first joined a Becoming Well Workgroup OR other recovery meeting? Maybe it caught you off guard, that people would come together to support each other. There is a safety that meetings provide, which cannot be found elsewhere.

When you share the reasons why you joined a recovery group, that darkest moment, that thing you thought you'd never share, you become freer. You begin recovering right there!

In a Becoming Well weekly meeting, you will be fully accepted while being fully known. Historically, many recovery groups offer this type of environment and expectation while maintaining confidentiality. Please see appendix____, where you can explore additional meetings to attend throughout the week in case you need them (e.g., workaholics anonymous, sexaholics anonymous, overeaters anonymous, etc.).

What brought you into Becoming Well meetings and how did it feel to share, be open, and be honest?

What do you gain from sharing openly and honestly with others?

When you are fully accepted and known by a higher power, how do you feel? Why?

Step 2 Connection: Explain how members in your meetings have displayed the character of a higher power to you.

PARTNER CONNECT Although you shouldn't share any specifics about what goes on in your confidential meetings, be sure to share the time and day of your meeting with your partner. Also, at the end of each meeting, note what you learned about yourself during that time. Share this with your partner every week, as it will help them trust you more if they understand that you are learning and growing.

 ## Exercise 4 — Phone Calls

Recovery is done together. We sharpen each other, accept each other, and praise one another throughout our battle with negative thinking, sexual struggle, moral failure, and unhealthy relationship habits. We choose to make a phone call for several different reasons. Here are some:

Reasons for Making a Phone Call

Welcome others into recovery * Share your story * Share burdens of recovery

Receive feedback * Process a Becoming Well Exercise * Ask questions about a Step

Process a negative thought about a partner * Process a temptation to act out sexually

Practice exercises for relational growth

Bookend the days/events/travel/situations when we know we will be tempted to avoid or act out

---

The goal is to make at least 6 calls each week. It's important to grow relationships during recovery. Isolation and secrets have broken down what we would want, which is a fulfilling life.

How have isolation and secrets hurt you and your relationships?

[ ]

Who are you able to talk with about your recovery? Make a list of trusted confidential people you can call, and write what makes them a safe person to talk with.

1.
2.
3.
4.
5.
6.
7.

Step (All) Connection: All of the steps have the word "we" in them.

Why is it beneficial for you to invest your time in making recovery phone calls?

[ ]

PARTNER CONNECT Share your answer to the question "how have isolation and secrets hurt you and your relationship?" with your partner. Have a discussion about how they see it.

90 in 90

Exercise 5

This exercise is particularly useful for those looking to recover from addiction.

Because intimacy avoidance is not considered an addiction but a way of thinking or state of mind, we are talking about 90 meetings in 90 days for those individuals looking to break free from the chains of sex addiction.

Alcoholics Anonymous (AA) coined the saying "It works if you work it," but how do you work recovery? Other than using this exercise book, you can go to meetings to form relationships with others in recovery. Meetings can help you heal from the shame of your sexual acting out, past and present.

"SA.org" and "Next Meeting for SA" are two locations online to join a meeting. You can be on the phone or video call within seconds. Listening to and sharing with a community that wants the same goal – freedom from lust and sexual addiction – is a tremendous help. The more support you have in the fight, the better. The fact is, people around the world are struggling and you are not alone. This collective community can also be found at local churches, Celebrate Recovery, Regeneration, and, of course, a Becoming Well Workgroup.

For your brain, sex is like a drug, stronger than heroin. That's why 3 months (90 days) is recommended to begin your sex addiction recovery with traction and in community.

Track your 90 meetings below

1	2	3	4	5	6	7	8	9	10
11	12	13	14	15	16	17	18	19	20
21	22	23	24	25	26	27	28	29	30
31	32	33	34	35	36	37	38	39	40
41	42	43	44	45	46	47	48	49	50
51	52	53	54	55	56	57	58	59	60
61	62	63	64	65	66	67	68	69	70
71	72	73	74	75	76	77	78	79	80
81	82	83	84	85	86	87	88	89	90

If you are willing to use this exercise, summarize what you will gain from attending meetings.

Steps 1-3 Connection: Write a recovery prayer or letter to your higher power, admitting your powerlessness over sexual temptation. Express your belief that this power can win the battle, and open your heart to its will for your life.

PARTNER CONNECT If you have committed to attending 90 meetings in 90 days, share this fact with your partner.

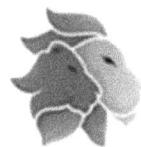# Exercise 6 — Choose a Sponsor

When you join a Becoming Well Workgroup OR recovery group, you will be meeting guys who are also recovering from sexual addiction, infidelity/betrayal, intimacy avoidance, or a combination of these. In this process of becoming honest, open, and vulnerable, you will be required to make phone calls as part of your weekly routine. This is where you need to start looking for your sponsor.

After you connect over the phone or video call, ask yourself: do they have experience in recovery, have they gone through similar struggles as me, and where are they at in mending and rebuilding trust with their partner?

Choosing a sponsor is an individual choice, and it's an important one. Your sponsor will be the first person you reach out to if you are in a negative mindset, tempted to act out in SA, or need someone to *Bookend* with. Of course, you will need to have more than one person to call in case your sponsor is unavailable.

Since joining your workgroup, who have you connected with? In what ways are you similar?

How will you benefit from having a sponsor? Why would a call with a sponsor help you grow and recover?

Choose! Ask a member of your workgroup to sponsor you in Becoming Well. Write why you chose them below.

Name_____

I chose them because…

Step 1 Connection: Explain how the concept of "We" is demonstrated in having a sponsor to support you.

PARTNER CONNECT Once you have chosen a sponsor, share that fact with your partner. You may share the first name of your sponsor with your partner, as well as the reason(s) you chose this particular person. Be careful that you don't divulge any private information about your sponsor to your partner.

30-Day Checklist

Exercise 7

Use this template to keep track of your recovery goals. The Appendix can direct you to the exercises that correspond to each column. P1/P2 = Exercise found in corresponding workbook, Part 1 or 2

Day	Daily Prayers or Asks	Daily Check In (P1)	Empathy Exercise (P1)	Gratitude List (P1)	Exercises (P1 or P2)	Phone Call (P1)	Cynical Script (P2)	Played Victim Y/N	Defend/ Explain (P1)	SA Relapse Y/N (P1)	IA Behavior Y/N (P1)	Lie Y/N (P2)
1												
2												
3												
4												
5												
6												
7												
8												
9												
10												
11												
12												
13												
14												
15												
16												
17												
18												
19												
20												
21												
22												
23												
24												
25												
26												
27												
28												
29												
30												

PARTNER CONNECT As you are going through your 30-day Checklist, ask your partner for input where appropriate. Pay special attention to these items: played the victim, defense, and IA behavior. Your partner's input here is crucial, as you may not always be aware when you're doing these things.

THE FOUNDATIONS OF RECOVERY - PART 1 GROUND ZERO

 **Exercise 8**   **Weekly Check-In**

The weekly check-in is based on 4 areas of recovery that must be given attention.

In your Becoming Well Workgroup, you will be reading through key questions to stay accountable and listen to others. Reflect on how you can give feedback in the form of a **praise** and a **sharpen**.

The check-in has the following sections:

1. Sobriety	This includes reporting sobriety and whether you are following the program's suggested tools for recovery. Here we recognize that the destruction from our addiction (SA) or ways of thinking/operating (IA) will destroy our relationships if we are not held accountable to others.
2. Relational Work	We report to our partners, asking them for feedback about how we are doing this week. This is an essential part of studying and learning about our partners. We strive to practice empathy, cease being defensive, and be honest with our partners to build trust. Additionally, you will report to the group how your partner rated the relationship and why. This is meant to help you draw closer to a state of connection and commitment with your partner.
3. Group Work	The group work section of the check-in is an accountability section that has you track the number of recovery phone calls and your daily practice of gratitude. We attend weekly groups to show consistency in our commitment to recovery. This is also a trust builder with our partners.
4. Book Work	Here is where you report on how often you have done step work or workbook exercises during the week. This section of accountability coincides with our recovery plan created in your *Daily Times for Recovery* exercise. If you make the time, it will be evident week to week.
5. Highs and Lows	In the final part of our check-in, we are given time to share the past week's most flawed and successful moments in our recovery and relationship.

*You must express being "open to feedback" or "not open to feedback" at the end of every check-in

Feedback	**Praise** When listening to a check-in, be prepared to encourage each other **Sharpen** Depending on where someone is struggling, give a suggestion or rhetorical question for them to consider

If you are looking to join a *Becoming Well Workgroup*, then why wait?

All Steps Connection: Read over all the steps. Name 3 steps for which you will need a workgroup community to help you recover, and why.

RECOVERY TOOL BOX

1. Step____Why…
2. Step____Why…
3. Step____Why…

PARTNER CONNECT In addition to completing your weekly check-in for group, you also need to read it to your partner and ask for their input. This should be done every week, preferably the day before your meeting. If you have an evening meeting, and it is ok with your partner, you can go through it with them that morning. Do not wait until the last minute and then claim that your partner didn't have time or didn't want to do it. The weekly check-in is your responsibility, and you are responsible for making sure that you create a safe environment that your partner wants to participate in.

Exercise 9 — 24-Hour Tell Policy

To build trust and maintain accountability, it is your responsibility to have a 24-hour tell policy and honor it. The policy must include any behavior that would be considered as acting out in your struggle or breaking trust with regard to what you have agreed to follow through with for the relationship, family, or partner.

If you break your sobriety from SA or cross any boundary, it is important to tell your partner as soon as possible. New trauma may ensue by keeping the truth from your partner, so it is best to tell them. In your mind, it may seem like you're saving them from pain by not telling them, but that is a lie. Secrets about our struggle will only hurt you and them in the long run. It is selfish to keep the truth from them.

Processing how you will tell your partner beforehand is wise. Also, by anticipating any feelings they may have, you can prepare to *Hear and Validate* your partner.

What boundaries are included in your 24-Hour Tell Policy? Agree with your partner about each area listed.

How do you think your partner would feel if you didn't tell them when you broke the policy? What is at stake?

On a phone call with another person in recovery, discuss each other's policies. What's the same/different?

Step 3 Connection: How has "your will" been destructive when it comes to hiding behaviors?

<u>PARTNER CONNECT</u> Complete this exercise with your partner. Be sure they are aware of the 24-Hour Tell Policy. Ask them what they do and do not want to know and take notes.

100% Responsible

Exercise 10

Blaming someone or something else for your behavior will stop you from healing and recovering. Being 100% responsible means that you take the weight of what your actions have done. Realize that feeling guilty is natural as you get started on your recovery. Avoiding your responsibility to your partner has caused pain and been destructive to the relationship.

You then have a choice: to feel sorry for yourself, or to move forward into actions that will help you recover. Your partner cannot take responsibility for you. Focusing on yourself and what you need to take responsibility for is the foundation of recovery.

Ask yourself, "Am I 100% responsible for the devastation I've caused and my recovery from it?" Yes___ No___

Recall a time when you avoided responsibility. How did your choice cause pain for others?

Your partner wants to feel safe. How is taking responsibility related to building safety for them?

Say, "I am 100% responsible and I can recover!" five times. Do you believe it? Why or why not?

Step 3 Connection: Write a recovery prayer, thanking your higher power for the will and strength to take responsibility.

PARTNER CONNECT Ask your partner for their input on how taking responsibility is related to them feeling safe. Write down what they say in the space provided (item 2 of the exercise).

 **Exercise 11**   **Rubber Band**

"Snapping out of Destructive Thoughts and Behaviors"

The rubber band is a positive punishment tool. It's adding something unpleasant to discourage unwanted behavior. It's retraining your brain.

For sex addiction, the snap of the rubber band would be for behaviors such as fantasizing, ogling (checking out), or any form of lust. This is very powerful when you follow the snap with the exercise *Pray to Humanize.* By treating those we objectify like humans we are no longer able to objectify them in that moment.

For intimacy avoidance, the snap of the rubber band would be for any cynical script your mind goes to about your partner. To combat this negative story about your partner, follow the rubber band snap with a praise about your partner from your *Gratitude List*.

The rubber band brings mindfulness about your behaviors. It reminds you how destructive your behavior is and how the behavior is not good for you. Diligent use of the rubber band is essential. Snapping immediately is the key to using the rubber band effectively. It sends the message to your brain that what you just thought is unhealthy, destructive thinking.

Be aware that snapping the rubber band in front of your partner can create unnecessary anxiety for them because they don't know why you snapped the rubber band. The *presence* of the rubber band, however, sends the message to your partner that you're serious about your recovery.

Why are you willing to commit to wearing the rubber band? Record the date you began wearing it.

Date___/___/___

My why is…

Write down as many situations you can predict where you will need to snap your rubber band. (SA or IA)

1.
2.
3.
4.
5.
6.
7.

RECOVERY TOOL BOX

Step 1 Connection: How is the rubber band connected to you being powerless over your struggle?

```
┌─────────────────────────────────────────────────────────────────┐
│                                                                 │
│                                                                 │
└─────────────────────────────────────────────────────────────────┘
```

PARTNER CONNECT Explain the reason behind wearing a rubber band to your partner. Ask them if they'd prefer not to see you snap it or if they're okay with it. If they're okay with it, don't hide the use of your rubber band from them.

Exercise 12 — Blockers and Accountability Software

There are many options for software and blockers. First, realize there is a difference between the two.

Blockers monitor activity and stop access to websites and apps that can be used to fuel sexual addiction. Software puts high accountability on the person in recovery because they know that all their activity is monitored.

We recommend choosing accountability software and an accountability partner who will receive notifications by text or email of your activity.

Common Software Used: Covenant Eyes, Accountable2You, and Ever Accountable

Common Accountability Partner Options: Pastor, Close Friend, Sponsor, or Spouse/Partner

*Partners may not want to be your SA accountability partner

The key is that your accountability partner must actually hold you to your commitment and be willing to ask the hard questions about what led you to your acting-out behavior in the first place. Accountability software serves as a door for deeper understanding of your addiction in the case of a relapse.

What is the purpose of accountability software for all your devices?

How will you and your partner grow closer if you add this layer of accountability to your SA recovery?

Step 1 Connection: How is accountability software related to accepting you're powerless over your SA?

PARTNER CONNECT Talk to your partner about your blockers and/or accountability software. In addition to your sponsor or recovery partner, ask your partner if they want to be added to the list of who sees your reports. If they don't, offer to ask your recovery partner or sponsor if they would be comfortable sharing your breaks in sobriety with your partner, should you dishonor your 24-hour tell policy.

Book Work

Exercise 13

We either make the time or we don't. Your recovery is going to take deliberate planning and actions to recover from years or even decades of Sexual Addiction and/or Intimacy Avoidance. This needs to be a daily commitment because, if your mind is set on recovery every day, then your actions towards your partner, family, friends, and yourself will begin to change.

You need to put in a small amount of time every day. Below is a week-by-week planner for when you can set aside time, and how much. Creating this and sharing it with your partner will show them how serious you are about recovery. It will give both of you a way to measure that seriousness.

For the partner, this is one of many ways you can rebuild trust. Maybe they have never seen you follow through on your recovery. Maybe they have only seen half efforts and half-truths from you, which has demonstrated a lack of commitment to recovery. Time is a factor that can communicate how hard you truly want to work. So make it a significant amount of time, around 20 minutes at least.

Next, what are you working on? The rhythm you'll want to have is based on what you are recovering from. This is the rule of 3 and 3. Day 1, read recovery book (SA/IA). Day 2, Exercise from this book. Day 3, step book around SA/IA recovery. Then repeat again for Days 4, 5 & 6. **Expectation 6/7 days of recovery.**

Rhythm: Book, Work book, Step book; Book, Work book, Step book, Day off.

Day	Time: From	Time: To	What I plan to work on
Monday			
Tuesday			
Wednesday			
Thursday			
Friday			
Saturday			
Sunday			

THE FOUNDATIONS OF RECOVERY - PART 1 GROUND ZERO

Step 1 Connection: Have you ever been able to manage a day-to-day routine for self-improvement and devotion to address your own brokenness? If so, how can you empower yourself to commit to a daily plan? What's at stake? If you haven't, then what is motivating you towards recovery and commitment to a daily plan?

PARTNER CONNECT Once you have completed your plan of action, share this with your partner for extra accountability. Remember, following through on your plan is a way to build trust with your partner. But beware: a lack of follow-through on your part will lead to more distrust!

HALT BS   Exercise 14

Whether your recovery involves sexual addiction or intimacy avoidance, this acronym can assist you. It represents daily feelings and pitfalls that can cause your emotions to fluctuate and dive you into negative coping mechanisms. The more of these you have at one time, the more likely you are to fall back into destructive behaviors or ways of thinking.

H.	Hungry	This involves not just how often you eat but how you eat
A.	Angry	Unchecked resentment or frustration can swell if not processed and shared
L.	Lonely	Avoiding interaction with your partner, family, and friends
T.	Tired	Quality, duration, and when you sleep or rest
B.	Bored	Time management, cultivating a rhythm of life, filling your time
S.	Stressed	How full is your plate? What do you do to de-stress?

(ALL Step Connection: We recover together)

There are a hundred different things you could do to keep your heart and body happy.

Make a plan for each area of health and share your plan with another in recovery.

Be willing to revise this plan as you go through recovery, so you can depend on what you need to maintain sobriety and health.

	Plan	Revisions
Hungry		
Angry		
Lonely		

THE FOUNDATIONS OF RECOVERY - PART 1 GROUND ZERO

Tired		
Bored		
Stressed		

PARTNER CONNECT Share your HALT BS plan with your partner.

Gratitude List

Exercise 15

It is important to battle the cynical script, the negative things you think about your partner or others. This kind of thinking diminishes any positive thinking. Being thankful and being critical or judgmental cannot happen simultaneously. This is why this exercise is essential for your recovery and healing.

First, think about your partner. They are who you are most responsible for thinking positively about and expressing your gratitude towards. Next, the most important individuals to practice this with are your children and family. Then, consider any friends, coworkers, or others who may have hurt you that you will have to practice showing gratitude towards.

Brainstorm who the people or groups would be that you can practice gratitude towards in the categories below.

Partner	
Kid/Family	
Friends	
Coworkers	
Others that have hurt you	

At the top of each column, fill in the 4 people/groups you will be writing gratitudes for during the next week. Then write 3 things you're grateful for about them each day.

Day	_____	_____	_____	_____
1				
2				
3				
4				

5				
6				
7				

Step 8 Connection: In order to have an "attitude of gratitude" you will need to rely upon your higher power to help you open your heart and change the way you see others. Write a prayer, inviting the higher power to change the old ways of thinking that have led you to think critically and judge others.

PARTNER CONNECT Share at least one of the gratitudes you wrote about your partner daily with them.

Bookending　　　　　　　　　　Exercise 16

Bookends hold things in place by standing before and after books on a shelf.

Similarly, this exercise is meant to create guardrails for entering any situation that challenges your recovery or sobriety. You make a call before and after the challenging event or situation.

Suppose you expect a situation in the coming week, hour, or day to be challenging. Can you think of a situation that will possibly tempt you sexually or challenge your intimacy with your partner? We know that in recovery it's not a matter of if, but when we will face challenges. We have a choice then: do we reach out, make a call, send a text, process the challenge with each other, pray for one another, and strengthen each other – or not? We are stronger together in community than we are isolated and alone.

At the end of the day, or rather at the beginning, you have a choice. So make the choice to use bookending for the next challenging situation you face.

Name 3 events or situations you WILL enter, where you would benefit from bookending:

Now, practice bookending. Like a journal entry, describe what you discussed, what you prayed with each other about, and how you benefited from using bookending.

Before	After
1.	1.
2.	2.
3.	3.

ALL Step Connection: "We" is a word used to emphasize a community of like-minded people seeking recovery. Explain why bookending could help you on your recovery journey.

PARTNER CONNECT Share what you learned about bookending and tell your partner who you are going to start bookending with. It is not necessary to share specific struggles that you need to bookend about.

12 Steps in a Year

Step 1

Exercise 17

We admitted we were powerless over our struggle and that our lives had become unmanageable

Goals

- Be honest with yourself.
  This is going to feel like a radical shift from how you once lived. You are no longer alone, and your struggle is something that you must share with others in order to heal.

- You are not in control.
  You want to begin the practice of letting go of thinking that you have control over how you act in your destructive coping strategies. You will discover certain daily practices of surrender, prayer, and boundaries that will help you in the fight against slipping back into destructive patterns.

- Share the burden of recovery.
  We join a recovery group with the hope that we can get help. That help first and foremost comes with making phone calls to others in recovery. The goal is 6-7 calls minimum per week. If needed, call more, whenever you are triggered into acting out. We can and will help each other find a better way to live.

Expectations

- Taking action on this road of recovery requires routines, boundaries, and daily exercises. Having the vision or desire to recover is not enough. Action, or believed behavior, is what your loved ones will see as evidence of your recovery, because action makes your vision of healing become possible.

- Temptations will become less extreme the longer your sobriety lasts. Others in your recovery group will inspire you to press on and get back up, even after a slip. Listen to their guidance and put their feedback into action.

Hurdles

- Giving up control can feel counterintuitive.

  The 12 steps are built on the understanding that we cannot overcome our struggle with our own willpower, alone.

- You may reach desperation, a thirst, a drive inside you when you begin surrendering the areas of your life that you need help in. Pride will get in the way.

- Recovery is a marathon, not a sprint. Take everything one day at a time. Healing for yourself and loved ones will not happen in one day but is progressive.

- Remind yourself that you are worth it. You are worth healing, and you are worth the help others will give you through these desperate times.

THE FOUNDATIONS OF RECOVERY - PART 1 GROUND ZERO

Set a personal Goal, describe an Expectation you have, and state a Hurdle you can foresee or have.

Goal:
Expectation:
Hurdle:

PARTNER CONNECT Sometimes our loved ones can see things that we aren't aware of or have overlooked. Once you have set a personal goal and defined an expectation and a hurdle, share these with your partner. Ask for their input. Is there anything they're seeing that you aren't? If so, write it down.

_____

_____

_____

Now go to or order then go to your Becoming Well Institutes "**The 12 Steps to Becoming Well from Sexual Addiction or Intimacy Avoidance**" and complete this step.

Step 2

Exercise 18

We came to believe that a power greater than ourselves could restore us to sanity

Goals

- You begin exploring who or what your higher power is and has been to you
- This is a searching and reflective time of recovery. In particular, your history with your higher power is something you should reflect on.
- You will share this transformative time in Step 2 through daily routines of accepting your feelings, anxieties, and fears in prayer and fellowship throughout your day.
- Building off of Step 1, there is a desperation for healing that you must carry with you throughout recovery. Therefore, make the daily choice to believe healing is possible through your higher power. This is a practice and action that you and you alone must choose.

Expectations

- Daily spiritual practices are essential to recovery
- AM, PM, and daily surrendering prayers are foundational parts of recovery. Expect to be required to check in about how these practices are going.
- Share all your heart with your higher power. Baring your thoughts, feelings, and temptations to your higher power is essential as you emerge from your old habits of hiding.

Hurdles

- Connecting to your higher power can be mysterious and foreign.
- Start with recovery, surrender, and gratitude prayers to your higher power.
- Seek others in recovery for advice and help with where to start. Remember it is one day at a time, one prayer at a time, and one choice at a time.
- Prayer can feel awkward and shameful following the weight of relationship destruction. Remember that your higher power hears you and wants healing for you. Your higher power doesn't want the avoidant behaviors that brought you into recovery to be the end of your story. Your higher power wants you to live a life of health and to have a victorious ending to your story.

What are your initial thoughts and feelings when you read, "We came to believe that a power greater than ourselves could restore us to sanity?"

_____
_____
_____
_____
_____

Set a personal Goal, describe an Expectation you have, and state a Hurdle you can foresee or have.

Goal:
Expectation:
Hurdle:

PARTNER CONNECT Share what you have learned about your Higher Power with your partner and explain how this helps you.

_____
_____
_____

Now go to or order then go to your Becoming Well Institutes "**The 12 Steps to Becoming Well from Sexual Addiction or Intimacy Avoidance**" and complete this step.

Step 3   Exercise 19

We made a decision to turn our will and lives over to the care of our higher power as we understand them

Goals

- This decision is not made in one day or in one minute, but every day, with every prayer, and with every phone-call cry for help as we live a different life from the one we lived before.
- We need to make and revise boundaries to keep us sober in our recovery whenever triggering situations arise.
- We live in fellowship, turning our lives over to our higher power. This will involve honest assessment of the areas in our lives that may be unhealthy.

Expectations

- Freedom is found in full surrender.
- Our weaknesses are where we begin turning our lives over in order to receive healing and newfound strength.
- This is when we get into the details of where we need to turn over control. Whatever way you withhold, you will need to examine anything and everything that you idolize and obsess over that takes the place of your higher power in your heart.
- Sharing any anxiety or hesitation with those further in recovery will aid you in Step 3.

Hurdles

- Turning over our lives could mean changing where we spend our time, money, and attention. The truths that your higher power will begin revealing to you about unhealthy habits, relationships, and entertainment can be hard to accept.
- Trusting in your higher power is easier said than done. This is a daily practice, and if done with honesty and submission, it will be a painful and rewarding battle won with your higher power by your side.
- Moving on without fully submitting your life and will implies you aren't ready to move into Step 4. So slow down. One day at a time, seek your higher power in prayer and turn to others for help. Remember, you are worth it!

Set a personal Goal, describe an Expectation you have, and state a Hurdle you can foresee or have.

Goal:
Expectation:
Hurdle:

PARTNER CONNECT Make a list of at least 3 things you need to turn over to your Higher Power. Ask your partner for help making this list. Also, share with your partner your goal date to complete this step and who you have designated as an accountability partner. If it is someone from group, be sure to share only the first name to honor confidentiality.

_____
_____
_____

Now go to or order then go to your Becoming Well Institutes "**The 12 Steps to Becoming Well from Sexual Addiction or Intimacy Avoidance**" and complete this step.

Step 4   Exercise 20

We made a searching and fearless moral inventory of ourselves

Goals

- This is where honesty gets put into action. Document and reflect on your past regarding:
    - Harms done to me
    - Harms done to others
    - My tendencies toward others
- We reflect upon how we acted out or withheld, why we acted out or withheld, and the feelings that we associate with the actions that we committed or that were done to us.

Expectations

- By listing out our history, we begin searching for full honesty with our higher power and others.
- We may need to add to our inventory as time passes.
- It is not necessary to disclose your inventory. Talking to a recovery coach, a therapist, or a trusted spiritual leader will create a safe space to vent feelings associated with revisiting the past.
- Disclosure in a marriage may be necessary BUT be sure to create plans for such a disclosure with appropriate planning and guidance. Use individual and couples' recovery counseling or coaching.
- Becoming Well providers are an option for help with this process. We can create a safe space for such a disclosure to happen with the least amount of pain possible.
- We have experience and are certified and trained, but we also know firsthand from our own history of recovery that disclosure can look many different ways for different couples. The key is to be honest to the extent that it will help your partner feel safe.

Hurdles

- Emotions are raw when listing your history of destruction. At this point, leaning on your higher power and recovery partners will be essential to overcome the inevitable grief you will feel while recording your inventory.
    - Have a list of people to call handy whenever you're working through your inventory.
- You may feel broken and not worthy of healing while listing out the pain you have caused others.
    - Return to the foundation of Steps 1, 2, and 3, and remind yourself that your higher power wants nothing less than to free you from your broken ways of thinking.
- Adjust your daily recovery prayers to grieve the pain and seek your higher power for the strength to live a life in full surrender.
- Seek others in recovery who have experienced the freedom from completing an exhaustive Step 4 inventory. This step can and should be thorough. Take your time, because it will be worth the effort.

Set a personal Goal, describe an Expectation you have, and state a Hurdle you can foresee or have.

> Goal:
>
> Expectation:
>
> Hurdle:

PARTNER CONNECT After you take your "fearless moral inventory," be sure to get input from your partner. Ask them to name 3 things they see in your character that you should work on. Does their list coincide with yours? Do they have input that is different from the things you thought of? Are they right? If so, write down what they told you.

_____
_____
_____

Now go to or order then go to your Becoming Well Institutes "**The 12 Steps to Becoming Well from Sexual Addiction or Intimacy Avoidance**" and complete this step.

Step 5

Exercise 21

We admitted to our higher power, to ourselves, and to others the exact nature of our wrongs

Goals

- This is where you become fully vulnerable – an open book – about your history, to your higher power and to others.
  - You will share your inventory with a recovery partner.
  - Disclosure to your significant other may be overdue and needed, so you will need to seek help in how to give a full disclosure. Becoming Well can help with that. So can any other trained recovery coach or counselor who specializes in disclosures.
- Admitting to your higher power is an ongoing process. Accepting the nature of your wrongs is an intimate process that starts with daily honesty with your higher power.
- Aim to fit time into your daily prayers and recovery work to speak light to your inventory, sharing it with your higher power.

Expectations

- Sharing your story will be freeing and uplifting. You will see a huge stride in momentum in your recovery during this step.
  - Keeping this momentum is important to be able to complete the 12-step process.
- The peace you feel from being open and honest, for maybe the first time ever, can be an exciting rush.
  - Therefore, that freedom is very personal. Others may not be feeling the freedom you are. They may expect you to remain under the pain they're still be experiencing.
- Whatever it is that you may have said to yourself, "I will take this to my grave" is exactly what you need to share with another and confess to your higher power. Your healing and recovery depend on it.

Hurdles

- Fear and secrecy can get in the way of being vulnerable and honest. The lies that your pain and addiction or avoidance will tell you can obstruct of your recovery and healing.
- As mentioned before, loved ones may negatively view your freedom and relief in being completely honest, especially anyone you have betrayed.
  - Be prepared to use tools to give space for their feelings of pain that persist or flare up. It is understandable for them to still feel pain.
  - If you need help understanding the other person's feelings, consult with a Becoming Well provider or other trained professionals.
- Always, always remember: you are worth recovery.

Set a personal Goal, describe an Expectation you have, and state a Hurdle you can foresee or have.

Goal:
Expectation:
Hurdle:

PARTNER CONNECT What was the biggest thing you learned from this step? Share that learning with your partner.

_____
_____
_____

Now go to or order then go to your Becoming Well Institutes "**The 12 Steps to Becoming Well from Sexual Addiction or Intimacy Avoidance**" and complete this step.

Step 6 — Exercise 22

We were entirely ready to have our higher power remove all these defects of character

Goals

- Here's where we become ready for change.
  - It may include giving up habits, attitudes, or ways of thinking.
  - Whatever the defect is that you identified in your inventory, your target in this step is to prepare your heart for putting those behaviors behind you.
- Be open to feedback and reflection.
  - If your actions are still a reflection of your defects, then you will need to be open to humility.
  - In this process, you may need to add to and record an ongoing inventory.

Expectations

- This step will consolidate and summarize the defects you identified in your inventory.
- You will need to share this process of summing up your flaws with others in recovery.
- Healing involves simply saying out loud that you are ready. Pray regularly, AM, PM, and throughout the day to prepare for your higher power to help you remove your character defects.

Hurdles

- Being ready for defects to be removed may involve removing unhealthy habits, pastimes, or relationships from your life.
  - Help from others in recovery and your higher power will reveal aspects of your life that need to be removed.
  - Removing your defects can be painful, like going into surgery. Exercises like appreciation and resignation letters can help with letting things go from your past.
- Seek guidance from others in recovery and hear how they became ready for their higher power to remove their character defects.
- Keeping true to daily submission, this is a one-day-at-a-time process. Let go and allow your higher power and others to help you prepare to move past your character defects and into a new life.

What are your initial thoughts and feelings when you read "We were entirely ready to have our higher power remove all these defects of character?"

_____
_____
_____
_____
_____

THE FOUNDATIONS OF RECOVERY - PART 1 GROUND ZERO

Set a personal Goal, describe an Expectation you have, and state a Hurdle you can foresee or have.

Goal:
Expectation:
Hurdle:

PARTNER CONNECT With your partner, share any hurdle you identified in completing this step. Tell them who you are going to be accountable to in order to overcome this hurdle.

_____
_____
_____

Now go to or order then go to your Becoming Well Institutes "**The 12 Steps to Becoming Well from Sexual Addiction or Intimacy Avoidanc**e" and complete this step.

Step 7

Exercise 23

We humbly asked our higher power to remove our shortcomings

Goals

- This is a process of practicing full surrender.
  - Create prayers to your higher power, asking them to remove your character defects.
  - Imagine what life would be like without your struggle
- Ongoing Inventory needs to be taken daily
  - When a defect arises, return to asking your higher power for its removal

Expectations

- Full recovery involves sharing your struggles with others. This is a key way to involve others and your higher power in the process of removal.
- Some keys to success are:
  - Trusting fully in your higher power.
  - Believing that your higher power can help.
- Strong emotion may rush out when you're imagining the removal of your defect.
- The feeling of desperation is good.
- Thirsting for a new way of living, provided by your higher power, is a gift.

Hurdles

- **This is the place where you've passed the halfway mark through the 12 steps, so don't give up!**
- Half efforts now will yield half results later.
- Practicing forgiving yourself, one defect at a time, and asking for their removal one at a time is how you begin to love yourself and, in turn, become able to love others fully.

What are your initial thoughts and feelings when you read "We humbly asked our higher power to remove our shortcomings?"

_____
_____
_____
_____
_____
_____
_____

Set a personal Goal, describe an Expectation you have, and state a Hurdle you can foresee or have.

> Goal:
>
> Expectation:
>
> Hurdle:

PARTNER CONNECT Identify at least one area where you think you're giving a "half effort" or less than a full effort. Share this with your partner and tell them who you are going to be accountable to in order to overcome this challenge.

_____
_____
_____

Now go to or order then go to your Becoming Well Institutes "**The 12 Steps to Becoming Well from Sexual Addiction or Intimacy Avoidance**" and complete this step.

Step 8   Exercise 24

We made a list of all people we had harmed, and we became willing to make amends to them all

Goals

- Reflect on all the people and organizations you wronged from your inventory.
- If you think of someone or some group you have missed, list them out as well in this step.
- Become clear on what making amends is and what it isn't.
- Have multiple discussions with those who have completed amends before. Take notes on how it went for them.
- Become willing by your higher power's strength, not your own. Surrender personal judgements and seek to forgive prior to entering an amends.

Expectations

- Amends Is NOT...
  - Expecting forgiveness from the person you harmed.
  - About sharing reasons for your struggles.
  - Placing blame for your struggles on traumas you've endured.
  - Expecting the other party to own their wrongs.
- Amends Is...
  - Communicating your faults and taking responsibility.
  - Recognizing the pain you have caused.
  - Asking for forgiveness.
- Becoming willing is another process involving prayer.
- Forgiving others for their wrongs frees you to be able to love them from this day on, whether they want to reconcile a relationship with you or not.

Hurdles

- Feelings can get in the way of making your amends
  - These include anger, resentment, pride, malice... basically anything that breeds a defensive or entitled stance.
  - Unforgiveness is at the root of your judgment towards someone. Forgiving them says, "I am handing their judgment over to my higher power."
- Becoming willing to make amends can look different depending on if a face-to-face amends will harm someone. Being willing to give a face-to-face amends is best, but Step 9 will explore other options.
- Owning up to your role in causing others pain can be frightening. Asking your higher power for the courage you need can be added to your daily prayers. Discuss such hesitancies with someone in recovery. Remember, you are worth it to your higher power and your loved ones to own your mistakes.

Set a personal Goal, describe an Expectation you have, and state a Hurdle you can foresee or have.

Goal:

Expectation:

Hurdle:

PARTNER CONNECT Your partner should be on your list for amends. Ask them to write you a letter explaining ways in which you have hurt them. Understanding specifics will help you as you prepare to make amends. You may not agree with everything in their letter. If you are struggling to see things from their point of view, ask one of your fellow group members, a coach, or a trusted friend to help you see things from their perspective.

_____
_____
_____

Now go to or order then go to your Becoming Well Institutes "**The 12 Steps to Becoming Well from Sexual Addiction or Intimacy Avoidance**" and complete this step.

Step 9

Exercise 25

We made direct amends to such people wherever possible, except when to do so would injure them or others

Goals

- Decide which people you can deliver an amends face-to-face to.
  - This will be a hard decision and will depend on whether or not giving a face-to-face amends will harm the person you have wronged, and whether or not they will want to receive your amends.
  - Counsel from others who have given their amends before is essential.
- Write amends to every person or group from your inventory whom you have harmed. This is a healing process for you.
- You will need to read your rough drafts to someone experienced in giving amends and make revisions.
- And finally, give your amends.

Expectations

- So here it is, a recipe for amends letter writing, RUT-ABC:
  - R - Recognize the Wrong
  - U - Understanding the Hurt
  - T - Taking Responsibility
  - A - Asking for Forgiveness
  - BC - Behavior Change
- You will use your inventory to direct much of this process. There is a lot of explanation for what Amends is, what it isn't, and what each part of RUT-ABC should look like.
- This process can take a substantial amount of time. It is understandable. Practice delivering the amends that are more challenging and prepare for the possible feelings the receiver may have.

Hurdles

- Their feelings may be centered on pain and anger.
  - Expect to stand under their feelings.
  - You will need to prepare for how they may react to you asking for forgiveness. If emotions are high, you may need to prepare some diffusing strategies. Seek counsel on such strategies from others more experienced at giving amends.
- Your higher power will be your strength through the amends-writing process and when you're giving the amends.
  - Your dependence upon your higher power will be tested.
  - You are worth owning your defects and how they have caused pain to others. Remember that giving your amends and moving towards reconciliation is going to strengthen your recovery and your relationship with your higher power.

Set a personal Goal, describe an Expectation you have, and state a Hurdle you can foresee or have.

Goal:
Expectation:
Hurdle:

PARTNER CONNECT It is crucial that you don't ask your partner to accept any responsibility for the things you have done. Make sure you have worked through any resentments you hold against your partner before making amends to them. Avoid making your amends about you in any way, including putting pressure on your partner to forgive you and/or "get over it." Check your needs at the door so that your amends can be as heartfelt as possible.

_____
_____
_____

Now go to or order then go to your Becoming Well Institutes "**The 12 Steps to Becoming Well from Sexual Addiction or Intimacy Avoidance**" and complete this step.

Step 10 — Exercise 26

We continued to take personal inventory and, when we were wrong, promptly admitted it

Goals

- From this point on, the end of this process is only the beginning.
  - The purpose of the 12 steps is to give you a new way to live your life. The primary way we do this in recovery is to have an open, honest, and ongoing personal inventory.
- Honesty is the goal, the main goal, the only goal in this step.

Expectations

- Your routines will begin to change.
  - Daily recovery work will begin evolving into fewer questions to answer in the step work and more reflection about everyday living.
- Immediately admitting you're wrong should be something you are practicing regularly already with weekly check-ins.
- Honesty has become a way of living now, and going back to secrecy needs to be a thing of the past.

Hurdles

- Temptation will always be present in your life of recovery.
  - The truth is that we all slip and are not perfect.
  - Secrecy will be a temptation that can set you back, returning to steps 1, 2, and 3.
- Remember the cost and destruction from your behaviors.
- This step is the launching point into lifelong healing and recovery. Even when the 12 steps are over, the fight isn't.
- You are worth a life of authentic relationships and freedom from your withholding behaviors.

What are your initial thoughts and feelings when you read "We continued to take personal inventory and, when we were wrong, promptly admitted it.?"

_____
_____
_____
_____
_____
_____

THE FOUNDATIONS OF RECOVERY - PART 1 GROUND ZERO

Set a personal Goal, describe an Expectation you have, and state a Hurdle you can foresee or have.

Goal:
Expectation:
Hurdle:

PARTNER CONNECT It is crucial for the health of your recovery that you take your inventory at the end of each day to identify any ways in which you have been wrong and/or hurt others. This week, ask your partner if there is anything you have said and done that they need you to apologize for.

_____
_____
_____

Now go to or order then go to your Becoming Well Institutes "**The 12 Steps to Becoming Well from Sexual Addiction or Intimacy Avoidance**" and complete this step.

Step 11

Exercise 27

We seek to improve contact with a higher power through prayer and meditation, praying for knowledge of that power's will for our lives and the strength to carry it out

Goals

- We started with relying upon a higher power, and we end with relying upon that higher power.
- Creating ongoing habits, devotionals, and meditations will center your life on a will greater than your own.
- Continue to build upon your current relationship with your higher power.

Claim a life of peace with your higher power as your provider, not people, not materials, not your past coping mechanisms.

Expectations

- Your spiritual walk is only as good as the effort you put into it.
  - This is your daily choice: whether to put your higher power or idols first in your heart.
- Surrendering your own will and seeking your higher power's will for your life is a practice, not a faucet or light switch.
- Whether in good times or desperate ones, you will continue to need to seek your higher power in order to seek ongoing recovery.

Hurdles

- Feelings are not always something to be followed:
  - Our own will gets in the way sometimes
  - Thinking you've got it under control will lead to arrogance and pride
  - Boasting will lead to self-centeredness
- Remember how your higher power has helped you in this walk of recovery. Your higher power will be what leads you into a life of humility and peace.

What are your initial thoughts and feelings when you read "We seek to improve contact with a higher power through prayer and meditation, praying for knowledge of that power's will for our lives and the strength to carry it out?"

_____
_____
_____
_____
_____

Set a personal Goal, describe an Expectation you have, and state a Hurdle you can foresee or have.

Goal:
Expectation:
Hurdle:

PARTNER CONNECT If prayer is a part of your daily life, ask your partner to join in prayer with you each day. If not, share with your partner what you have been learning about daily interactions with your higher power.

_____

_____

_____

Now go to or order then go to your Becoming Well Institutes "**The 12 Steps to Becoming Well from Sexual Addiction or Intimacy Avoidanc**e" and complete this step.

Step 12   Exercise 28

Having had a spiritual awakening from our experience through the steps, we seek to share with others and practice our principles in all our relationships

Goals

- Pray for your higher power to use you, and to open doors to what may come next in your walk of recovery.
- Assess the season you're in.
- Stay connected with others in recovery even after commencing.
- Commencement means you aren't finished yet and will always be in the process.

Expectations

- You can develop purpose for your life in recovery.
    - A higher power can use you and your story to impact the lives of others if you allow it.
    - Relationships with those seeking a better, freer life from struggles will be more vulnerable and loving.
- Behaviors that you keep and take with you will be the evidence of real change.

Hurdles

- Closing yourself off to your higher power or their purposes can feel tempting.
    - Keeping your story to yourself.
    - Thinking you got this now on your own.
    - Resorting to old habits out of resentment from lost relationships.
- Remember that your higher power wants a new life for you. You are worth lifelong healing and recovery.
- With the progress you've made, practice gratitude, and use any exercise up until this point whenever you need.
- Keep going, keep relying, keep believing that you are worth it!

What are your initial thoughts and feelings when you read "Having had a spiritual awakening from our experience through the steps, we seek to share with others and practice our principles in all our relationships?"

_____

_____

_____

_____

Set a personal Goal, describe an Expectation you have, and state a Hurdle you have or can forsee.

Goal:
Expectation:
Hurdle:

PARTNER CONNECT Share with your partner the name of at least one person you plan to share your story with.

_____
_____
_____

Now go to or order then go to your Becoming Well Institutes "**The 12 Steps to Becoming Well from Sexual Addiction or Intimacy Avoidance**" and complete this step..

Helping My Partner Heal
(Part 1)

Rebuilding Trust Pyramid – Honesty

Exercise 29

The first layer of the rebuilding trust pyramid is honesty. Honesty is the foundation of trust in all healthy relationships. Without honesty, relationships fail to thrive. When we work with wounded partners, they often tell us that the lies they were told by the wounding partner are just as hard, if not harder, to move past than the betrayal-related behavior. Lying, for most wounded partners, represents multiple betrayals. These betrayals often make them feel disrespected and foolish. Not only did the wounding partner break the agreement between the couple when they engaged in the betrayal-related behavior, but they lied about it. This causes the wounded partner to call into question everything that happened before and after the lies were told.

If honesty cannot be established, what remains is a relationship devoid of trust and intimacy.

If a couple is to have a chance at rebuilding their relationship after betrayal, it must be built on a foundation of honesty and transparency. Ongoing lying and dishonesty will send the wounded partner the message that the wounding partner is primarily concerned with their own comfort, even if it is at the expense of the wounded partner's heart.

Step 1 Connection:

a. In your own words, why is honesty the foundation of your relationship(s)?

b. Name three topics you recall in the past where your lying was automatic, a powerlessness to protect yourself.

1.	2.	3.

PARTNER CONNECT Honesty is not only foundational to a trusting relationship with your partner; it is foundational to your personal recovery as well. Honesty fosters intimacy, but it also helps with self-awareness. It holds us accountable to ourselves, too. When we are dishonest with others, we are first dishonest with ourselves. When we break trust with others by being dishonest, we break trust with ourselves. Shame is a major reason we are dishonest. Something you can do with your partner to help you reduce shame is the "Worst Moment of the Day" exercise. If your partner is willing, add this exercise to your dailies. It's simple: tell your partner one moment of the day that was your worst moment. A moment when you weren't proud of how you behaved or what you thought. (Be careful that you don't tell your partner something bad you thought about them, as this will hurt them and cause discord.) If they are willing, they will listen to what you said and say, "Thank you for telling me. I love you anyway."

Rebuilding Trust Pyramid – Safety

Exercise 30

When we speak with wounded partners who have been hurt by their partner's betrayal-related behavior, they almost always describe feeling unsafe. First and foremost, this is because the predictability of the relationship is now gone. This typically initiates a fight-or-flight response from the wounded partner because the wounding partner's actions have caused betrayal trauma. Unfortunately, it can take the wounded partner weeks and months (in some cases longer) before their body and mind stop reacting to the trauma. Safety in the relationship must be re-established if the wounded partner is ever to get out of a hypervigilant mode of operation. In the case of relationships where intimacy avoidance is present, safety may never have been properly established in the first place.

When betrayal occurs, it can cause a lack of safety in several areas. The **types of safety** that are most often violated are physical/sexual, emotional, and commitment. Fill out the blank below to determine and understand the type of safety your wife/partner is requesting:

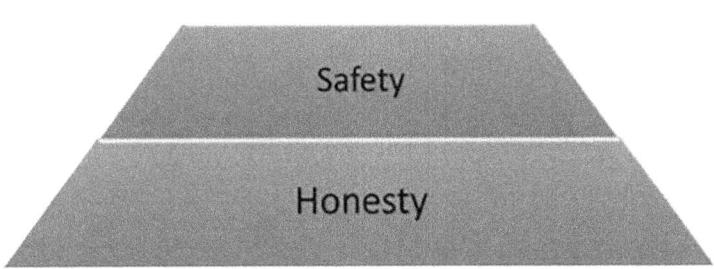

"My wife says she needs _____ to feel safe."

Some more examples: She needs: your attention, you to stop lying, to communicate with her better or more, to be more vulnerable, to be heard, you to be consistent, to install a tracking app on your phone, respect, to stop sexually pressuring her, transparency, honesty, to look at your phone, reassurance, emotional support, to share your struggles.

In the table below, name the "area" where you have created a lack of safety (use the **types of safety** listed above) and name an action to begin creating safety. Call others who are further along in recovery about their experiences and ideas for creating safety. Discuss your ideas with your partner as well.

Types of Safety	Plan of Action

PARTNER CONNECT Once you have completed the exercise, share it with your partner. Ask them if they have further input. If they do, add what they say to your exercise.

Rebuilding Trust Pyramid – Consistency

Exercise 31

The third layer of the rebuilding trust pyramid is consistency.

Consistency is an important ingredient in trust because it shows the wounded partner that they can depend on the wounding partner to follow through. When we work with couples to develop plans to create safety, we always explain that, without consistency, those plans are basically useless. When the wounding partner engages in infidelity-related behavior, they send a message to the wounded partner that they can't be trusted to uphold the promises and agreements that are important to the health of the relationship. If the wounding partner wants their partner to accept that they can change this, they must be consistent.

What is going to show Consistency to your partner?

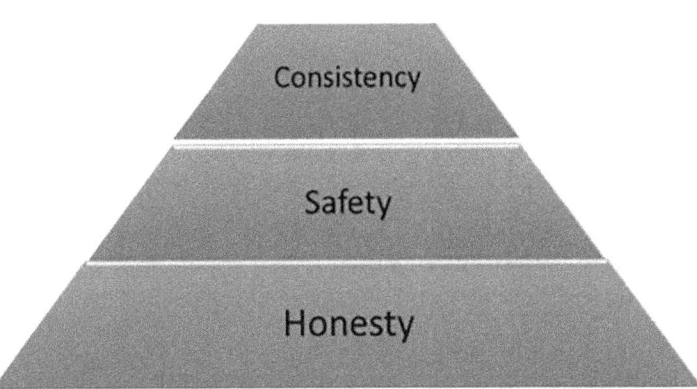

Here's a place to start:

1) Refer to any exercise you have done so far in The Becoming Well Workgroup program
2) Refer to the past two exercises on safety and honesty
3) Refer to others in recovery, asking them what evidence of consistency there has been in their relationship
4) Create consequences for yourself (e.g. No electronic devices for a week, 25 push-ups, eat an onion…)

Consistency Behavior	Day(s) of the Week	My Consequence if I Don't Follow Through or Reward if you do
	M T W Th F Sa Su	
	M T W Th F Sa Su	
	M T W Th F Sa Su	

	M T W Th F Sa Su	
	M T W Th F Sa Su	
	M T W Th F Sa Su	
	M T W Th F Sa Su	

PARTNER CONNECT Designate at least one person to whom you are going to be accountable for your plan. Share this exercise with your partner for extra accountability.

Rebuilding Trust Pyramid – Intimacy

Exercise 32

The fourth and final layer of the rebuilding trust pyramid is intimacy. When we think of intimacy, people tend to jump straight to sex. Although this is one type of intimacy and is often an expression of other types, it is not the only one.

Some common areas of intimacy that a couple can share are created by:

- sharing emotions
- resolving conflict successfully
- sharing goals and dreams
- sharing and respecting each other's thoughts and opinions
- connecting around religion and spiritual ideas and beliefs, and
- sharing hobbies and interests.

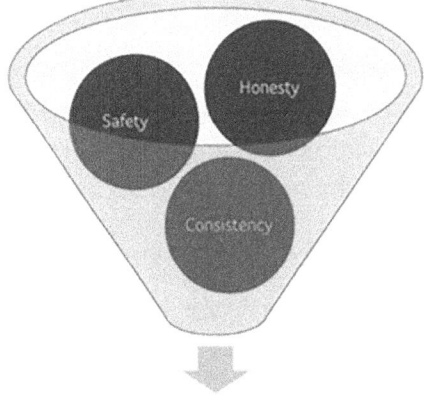

The feelings of devastation, betrayal, loneliness, ambivalence, and confusion caused by betrayal cause a breakdown in intimacy between partners. One of the reasons for this is that these feelings can cause one or both parties in the relationship to withdraw. Although this is common for a period when infidelity is discovered or disclosed, both partners will need to recommit to the relationship if trust is to be restored.

In the case of relationships where intimacy avoidance is present, little to no intimacy was present in the relationship prior to the discovery or disclosure of betrayal.

When we test couples for the strength of their relationship structures, we typically find that most of these are completely missing. The issues caused by intimacy avoidance and self-centered behavior leave the relationship weak. Adding betrayal to this already weak structure makes it extremely difficult for couples dealing with these issues to survive, unless the intimacy avoidant is willing to admit the totality of their bad behavior and begin recovery right away.

Intimacy will be built all along the recovery journey, and the "ingredients" of honesty, safety, and consistency are what produce intimacy.

Sign and date here to make a commitment to a higher power, your partner, your family, and yourself, that you will work to consistently create safety and trust in your relationship.

I, _____(name), commit on _____(date).

Signature_____

<u>PARTNER CONNECT</u> Ask your partner what types of intimacy they feel are most lacking in your relationship. Make a plan with your partner to address their top 2 intimacy concerns.

 # Exercise 33   Standing Shoulder to Shoulder

Why is it important for us to stand shoulder to shoulder with our partner in their pain?

As the wounding partner, one straightforward reason is that we've created quite a bit of pain for the wounded partner.

Our partner is in pain for lots of different reasons. In the beginning of the couple's recovery process, we're mostly standing shoulder to shoulder and helping them to heal from the pain that we've created. As we help our partners heal from much of the pain that we've caused, they start sharing other areas of their life where they've experienced or are currently experiencing pain.

So how do we stand shoulder to shoulder with our partner in their pain?

We use the *empathy exercise.*

We use *speaker-listener strategies* to make sure that they know that we're hearing them.

We set aside time on a weekly basis to have them share their pain with us so that we can help them process it.

We decide that we're going to be a healing agent, not a re-wounding agent, as they share pain with us.

We investigate and hear what they're saying rather than defending or refuting it.

All these are tools in this exercise book. We lean into the storm rather than run away from it.

Review the exercises in this book or other programs you've entered to help your partner heal and complete an "I will…" sentence for each.

I will…

I will…

I will…

I will…

HELPING MY PARTNER HEAL (PART 1)

I will…
I will…
I will…
I will…
Use more paper if needed

Early in recovery, as well as throughout recovery, we stand shoulder to shoulder with our partners. This means choosing to stand with our partners as they're going through the pain rather than creating more pain for them or abandoning them in their pain.

What days each week can you set aside to go to your partner and say, "is there anything that's happened to create pain for you for you?"

When our partner does bring their anger, complaints, or sadness to us, the key is to be purposeful and intentional.

To stand shoulder to shoulder, you need to not defend, explain, or correct them.

To stand shoulder to shoulder, you must learn to put yourself in their shoes (empathy).

Standing shoulder to shoulder with them does not mean that you agree with what they're saying, or that what they're saying is completely accurate, as that's not relevant. What is relevant is that they're experiencing pain, and you must show you care about them and want to help.

What pain statements have they made recently? How about in the past year? How can you can stand with them shoulder to shoulder?

Step 8 Connection: Write a prayer to open your heart to hear your partner's pain and bear it with them, and the patience to hear it without defending, explaining, or offering advice. Write this prayer on a flash card. As you get home from work or return to your partner, you can prepare your demeanor to engage with your partner in love and kindness.

PARTNER CONNECT Share your answers to steps one and two of this exercise with your partner.

Demeanor - Part 1

Exercise 34

Until the wounded partner feels a great deal of safety within the relationship, little-to-no progress will be made toward rebuilding trust. One of the main ways that safety can begin to be reestablished — or established for the first time, in the case of an intimacy avoidant relationship — is through the demeanor of the wounding partner.

If the wounding partner continues to be resistant to recovery or acts prideful, defensive, and/or arrogant, the wounded partner will not feel safe enough to engage in the recovery of the relationship. It is not enough to end the betrayal-related behavior, although this is extremely important.

The wounding partner also needs to be able to show true remorse for their actions. Arrogance, pride, and defensiveness send the wounded partner the message that the wounding partner is not truly sorry for what they have done and/or does not understand the effect that their actions have had on their partner.

When a wounding partner engages in infidelity-related behavior, they selfishly set the wounded partner aside in favor of something else. As a result, the wounded partner feels disrespected, unimportant, and forgotten. This is why it is of the utmost importance that the wounding partner show that they will do whatever it takes to win their partner back.

If the wounding partner continues to display a lack of humility by acting defensive, arrogant, or prideful, they inadvertently convey the message to the wounded partner that they should not ask for what they need in order to heal. Instead, they should just be happy with whatever the wounding partner is willing to give.

A defensive, prideful, or arrogant demeanor on the wounding partner's part sends the message that they do not value their partner. Someone with this type of demeanor needs to ask themselves why anyone would want to stay with someone who shows them this type of disrespect.

Why should anyone stay with a person who could cast them aside in an act of unfaithfulness and then continue to act remorseless about it and/or protect their own self-interest? When we view things in this light, we begin to understand how gracious the wounded partner is being by offering the wounding partner another chance.

What does it look like to show remorse?

Exercise: Look in the mirror. Display remorse with your posture, body language, and facial expression. Hold this position and picture the feelings your partner has.

What feelings do you have about the devastation you've caused?

Step Connection: What actions do you do on a day-to-day basis to show your partner an understanding, caring, and empathic demeanor?

```
┌─────────────────────────────────────────────────────────────────────────┐
│                                                                         │
│                                                                         │
└─────────────────────────────────────────────────────────────────────────┘
```

PARTNER CONNECT   With your partner, take the 5 Apology Languages Quiz at https://5lovelanguages.com/quizzes/apology-language. Have a discussion with your partner regarding what makes an apology meaningful to them. Take notes and put what they told you, along with your own answers, in the box designated "What does it look like to show remorse?"

70/30 to 80/20

Exercise 35

In our work, we've found that when couples come to us, the wounding partner – the person who's bringing the sexual betrayal, the intimacy-avoidant behavior, etc. – is usually bringing 70% to 80% of the problems in the relationship.

Does the other partner bring problems and pain to the relationship? Absolutely. However, all pain is not created equal. In using relationship-ending behaviors and ways of thinking, the wounding partner's percentage to take responsibility for is much greater.

Here's the good news if you're in a relationship like this, where you are responsible for most of the relationship problems. You can heal 70 to 80% of the struggles in the relationship. That means that you can bring the relationship to a B or a C grade just by doing your part.

Think of it as first, second, third, and fourth gears. You need to keep it in first gear, which is working on yourself, and second gear, which is making things safe for your partner. This is a part of your 70 to 80% recovery work.

Reflect on your recovery so far. What actions are you taking that is evidence of you taking responsibility?

What behaviors do you need to improve or begin in order to reach a B or a C grade for the relationship?

Step 5 Connection: On a recovery call this week, confess these areas you need to be held accountable for. Ask them how they are doing. Make this kind of accountability a normal part of your weekly calls.

PARTNER CONNECT At a time when things are calm, ask your partner what you could do better to take accountability for ways you have hurt the relationship. Make sure you are prepared to hear what they have to say without defending yourself or getting angry. You can do this by making a recovery phone call ahead of time. After you have listened to your partner's point of view and validated their experience, make a recovery phone call to help yourself process what they have said to you.

 # Exercise 36 — Stabilization

We use the term "stabilization" to describe a phenomenon common to intimacy-avoidant relationships.

Let's pretend that your relationship is on a scale. On this scale, positive 4 represents the closest you can be with your partner emotionally, while -4 represents the furthest away you can be emotionally from your partner. Intimacy avoidants are uncomfortable with emotional closeness. As a result, they tend to keep the relationship at about a -1. The partner is unhappy enough to keep their distance, but not so dissatisfied that they want to leave.

Over time, IA behavior begins to "move the needle" on relationship satisfaction. The other partner starts to become more and more disgruntled. Their unhappiness moves them to a -2, then a -3, and so on. They soon become so unhappy that they start threatening to end the relationship.

The IA, not wanting to be abandoned, suddenly starts to do recovery work. They take their partner out on dates, start to share emotions, spend more quality time, etc. In other words, they start doing everything their partner has been asking for all along. As a result, the partner begins to feel safe and loved. They stop threatening to leave the relationship.

The IA, sensing that the danger of abandonment has passed, gradually stops putting in the effort. Things go back to the way they were. The emotional distance is comfortable for the IA, so they are satisfied. The partner is not. The cycle starts all over again. This is highly emotionally damaging to a partner. There are only so many cycles that a partner can stand before they exit the relationship permanently.

The sad thing is that the stabilization cycle has nothing to do with the IA helping their partner heal. It has everything to do with making the relationship less painful for themselves. Whether it's the avoidance of abandonment or simply getting tired of hearing their partner's complaints, the IA engaged in stabilization is making selfish choices when it comes to recovery.

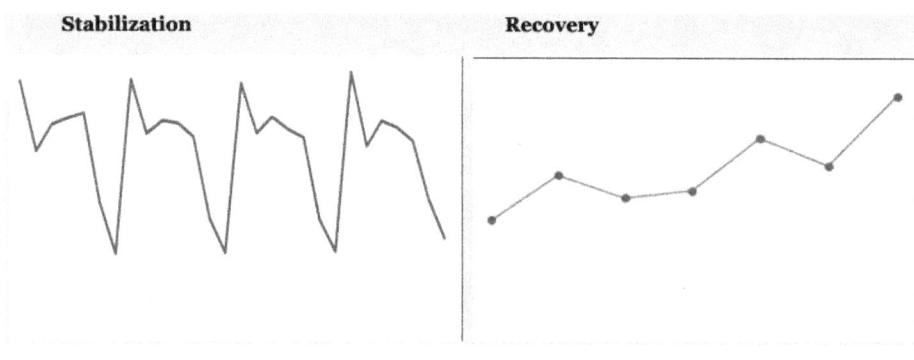

The two graphs represent the difference between stabilization and true recovery. If you look at the stabilization graph, you can see highs and lows. However, if you draw a line of best fit across the peaks of the graph, you can see that it's a flat line. The relationship is going nowhere. The "highs" only feel like progress because the lows hurt so much. The pain of emotional distance is only temporarily relieved, only to start all over again. This is not recovery.

If you look at the recovery graph, you can see that it looks quite different. Although highs and lows are represented on the graph, the line of best fit would show an upward trajectory. This graph represents consistent effort. Although there will be times when you aren't perfect (represented by the lows), you and your relationship will be making progress overall. This is true recovery.

HELPING MY PARTNER HEAL (PART 1)

How are you currently stabilizing your partner? If not, then what evidence do you have that you're in recovery?

When have you stabilized your relationship?

What needs did you meet for your partner that, once the relationship was stabilized, you stopped?

What did you prioritize over staying consistent in recovery?

Step 9 Connection: While being up and down about recovery, write a sentence Recognizing the Wrong, Understanding the Pain, and Taking Responsibility (RUT) for your lack of consistency.

R -

U -

T –

PARTNER CONNECT Explain this exercise to your partner. Ask them if they resonate with it. Ask them if they think you are still doing it. Take note of what they say so that you can identify ways to improve.

Emptying the Pain Closet   Exercise 37

We became the wounding partner through sexual betrayal and intimacy avoidance-related attitudes and behaviors. We have created many different sizes and intensities of pain for our partners, whom we call the wounded partner.

It's like our partners have this big pain closet and, in that closet, there are many different sizes of pain containers. Many of these pains, we created, and others we didn't. Regardless, our behavior has made all their pain harder to bear.

As the wounding partner, we must decide to help our wounded partner empty their pain closet.

How do we help them empty their pain closet? What do they need daily to feel safe enough to empty it?

[ ]

Again, connected to standing shoulder to shoulder with our partners in their pain – as well as staying connected to hearing, validating, and empathizing with their pain – we must commit to helping them empty the pain closet. We must be intentional about it.

What will you do this week to help unpack a container of their pain?

[ ]

Many times, men say that women never forget. I would challenge that. I'd say that there's a good chance that it's not that she doesn't want to forget, but she's never gotten the opportunity to process the pain that would allow her to let it go.

We have found in our practice at Becoming Well that when partners were able to process their pain containers, most of those containers went away and never came back.

Some pain containers are so hurtful on so many different levels that it takes a lot of time and effort and multiple conversations to process. But that deep pain container can be taken out of the closet.

THE FOUNDATIONS OF RECOVERY - PART 1 GROUND ZERO

Step 9 Connection: Complete this statement as many times as they have pain containers:

"My partner has pain from_____ and I am responsible for _____ about that container."

PARTNER CONNECT To complete section one of the exercise, please ask your partner what would help them empty their pain closet and what they need from you to feel safe enough to share this with you.

Empathy Exercise

Exercise 38

Empathy Exercise

This is a combination of several communication tools, including Dr. Doug Weiss's understanding exercise, the speaker/listener exercise from the book *Fighting for your Marriage*, and other adaptations to increase the effectiveness of this extremely helpful tool.

There are 6 steps to effectively using this tool with a couple of pre-steps.

Step 0 – Self Regulate

Step 0 – Demeanor Check

Step One: Get to the Heart of the Matter

Step one will start with what we call a "**pain statement.**"

- The point of step one is that no matter the statement, your job is to get under it and **find the source of the pain**.
- **Don't Defend. Explain and correct.**
- Using the **speaker/listener technique**, let your partner talk.
    - **REMINDER**: You are using the speaker/listener technique *ONE WAY*. When using this exercise, it is not your turn.
    - *If you make it about you, you will undermine the whole experience.*

Speaker Rules:

1. Speak only for yourself
2. Be respectful
3. Keep your statements brief and to the point
4. Stop frequently to let the listener repeat what you said

Listener Rules:

1. Repeat what you heard by saying, "what I heard you say is _____. Is that correct?"
2. If you weren't correct with what you repeated, speaker should say "no" and say it again.
3. Keep repeating this process until you get what they said correctly.
4. Once you repeat what they said correctly, ask, "is there more?"
5. DO NOT rebut.

Step Two (Part A): Discover and Explore Your Partner's Feelings

- Once you have gotten to the heart of the matter, ask them to express how the situation has them feeling. You can ask questions such as, "how does that make you feel?" or "how do you feel about that?"
- **Hint: This is another place where it is useful to use the Speaker/Listener Technique to repeat what your partner has told you. This will make sure you understand what they are trying to say before moving on.**

Step Two (Part B):

- Once your partner has expressed their feelings, pause for a moment. Imagine a time when you felt similarly. What happened? How did it affect you? Did it have lasting effects?

Step Three: Validate Your Partner's Feelings

- "It makes sense that you could feel that way." This requires empathy. You're putting yourself in your partner's shoes and moving from your self-centered perspective to your partner's perspective.

If they are still escalating, you missed something and need to go back.

Step Four: Take Responsibility

In this step, there are only two acceptable responses:

1. "Yes, I did that." (If you did it, own it.)
2. "I don't know if I did that this time, but I definitely have done that in the past. I can see why you would think that I did it and feel the way you feel about it."

Step Five: Ask Your Partner What They Need

Ask your partner what they need from you. Remember, it's not helpful to evaluate what they need or interject with what you think they need or should need. Just accept it.

Step Six: Just Do It

List out at least 3 common pain statements where your partner is expressing deep pain, anger, and sadness about your actions/inactions.

1.

2.

3.

When your partner is in pain and expressing it to you, how do you feel?

Next to each feeling, what actions do you tend to take, almost without thinking about those actions?

What are the results of these actions/inactions? Name three scenarios below.

Feelings	Actions/Inactions	Results

HELPING MY PARTNER HEAL (PART 1)

Use this page to track using the Empathy Exercise for the next 90 days.

Beneath each day, write the feeling your partner is having and why they are having it.

Day 1	16	31	46	61	76
2	17	32	47	62	77
3	18	33	48	63	78
4	19	34	49	64	79
5	20	35	50	65	80
6	21	36	51	66	81
7	22	37	52	67	82
8	23	38	53	68	83
9	24	39	54	69	84
10	25	40	55	70	85
11	26	41	56	71	86
12	27	42	57	72	87
13	28	43	58	73	88
14	29	44	59	74	89
15	30	45	60	75	90

Step 2 Connection: Do you believe a power greater than yourself can restore your relationship? Write a prayer below that can help you self-regulate. Check your demeanor from any time prior to hearing your partner's pain, or even from in the middle of hearing their pain.

PARTNER CONNECT As instructed in the exercise, please practice the Empathy Exercise with your partner for the next 90 days. Be sure to track your progress.

No Defend Challenge – 13 Weeks

Exercise 39

For the next 13 weeks, keep track each day of whether you defended, explained, or corrected your partner in conversation or conflict. Each day you do, your consequence will be 25 push-ups*.

Choose to use the **empathy exercise** instead. Keep track as well!

Week 1	M	T	W	T	F	S	S
Defend/Explain							
25 Push-Ups							
Understanding Exercise							

Week 2	M	T	W	T	F	S	S
Defend/Explain							
25 Push-Ups							
Understanding Exercise							

Week 3	M	T	W	T	F	S	S
Defend/Explain							
25 Push-Ups							
Understanding Exercise							

Week 4	M	T	W	T	F	S	S
Defend/Explain							
25 Push-Ups							
Understanding Exercise							

Week 5	M	T	W	T	F	S	S
Defend/Explain							
25 Push-Ups							
Understanding Exercise							

Week 6	M	T	W	T	F	S	S
Defend/Explain							
25 Push-Ups							
Understanding Exercise							

Week 7	M	T	W	T	F	S	S
Defend/Explain							
25 Push-Ups							
Understanding Exercise							

Week 8	M	T	W	T	F	S	S
Defend/Explain							
25 Push-Ups							
Understanding Exercise							

Week 9	M	T	W	T	F	S	S
Defend/Explain							
25 Push-Ups							
Understanding Exercise							

Week 10	M	T	W	T	F	S	S
Defend/Explain							
25 Push-Ups							
Understanding Exercise							

THE FOUNDATIONS OF RECOVERY - PART 1 GROUND ZERO

Week 11	M	T	W	T	F	S	S
Defend/Explain							
25 Push-Ups							
Understanding Exercise							

Week 12	M	T	W	T	F	S	S
Defend/Explain							
25 Push-Ups							
Understanding Exercise							

Week 13	M	T	W	T	F	S	S
Defend/Explain							
25 Push-Ups							
Understanding Exercise							

After 13 Weeks

Total times I defended: ☐
Total Push-ups Completed: ☐
Total times I Understood: ☐

If you are unable to perform a push-up then:

a. Perform half push-ups
b. Or for health reasons, consider an alternative consequence that involves physical exertion.

Daily Check In

Exercise 40

The next two pages are to be used on a daily basis as options for checking in with your partner. Use these pages as a guide for both of you. Agree ahead of time to follow these steps to the best of your ability. Over time, after you've had enough practice, work towards sharing without having these pages as a guide. Choose one, FANOS or Safer Check-In, to see which fits your relationship needs.

"FANOS" Check In

Here is a quick look at what FANOS is. Each letter is an aspect of your inner life that you will share with your significant other.

- **F**eelings: Share an emotion you experienced today. Use a list of feelings or The Feelings Wheel at first as you build an emotional vocabulary.
- **A**ffirmations/**A**ppreciations: This is a positive word for your partner for who he/she is. Tell him/her something you appreciate that he/she has done today.

This is "you are _____" and "I appreciated it when you _____."

- **N**eeds: Tell your partner something you need from him/her. This could be a need you just recognized or one you have mentioned before that still has not been met. Don't skip this one. Sometimes you may have to think for a minute before you can verbalize what you need.
- **O**wnership: What have you done wrong that you need to take ownership of? This can be one of the most healing and connecting points.
- **S**truggles/**S**obriety: Agree together beforehand on what struggle/sobriety topic each person will discuss. It can be any number of things. Some examples are your sobriety date, recovery work, your diet, exercise, raging, perfectionism, criticizing, compulsively checking up on your partner, or defensiveness. If you are an addict, you need to focus on sobriety and recovery work.

When sharing FANOS:

- One person goes through the entire FANOS, and then the other person goes through the entire FANOS.
- Talking through the entire FANOS should take no longer than two minutes. You do have time to do this! I don't care how tired you think you are, you have four minutes to connect with your significant other.
- When you listen to FANOS, your role is not to give feedback or fix. Your role is simply to listen and be present. This is an important opportunity to share safety and love.
- If you want to respond to something your partner said in his/her FANOS, wait until the next day. Actually, responding the next day can be a good sign that you were listening, you have been thinking about it, and you care about what was shared.

Here is an example FANOS:

- **F**eelings: I'm a little scared but hopeful about what is going on with our children. I feel overwhelmed by work and the kids' schedule. I feel determined to finish the project in the yard this weekend. I felt relaxed today when we were watching a movie together.
- **A**ffirmation/**A**ppreciation: I appreciate that you took out the trash like you said you would. Thank you for putting gas in the car and always keeping the car fueled.

- **N**eeds: I need for us to have more time together, like the time we spent on the couch tonight watching the movie.
- **O**wnership: I own that I did speak angrily to you when you asked me to go to the store. You did not deserve that and I apologize for that.
- **S**truggles/**S**obriety: I felt a tug to be defensive today when you told me that you wanted me to do the laundry, but I checked myself at the time.

REMEMBER, this is NOT a time to give feedback, criticize, correct, or shame one another. Simply listen to each other and know that the goal of this exercise is to build intimacy and restore trust. The key to this sharing time is to create safety while demonstrating connectedness, accountability, and acceptance.

The "SAFER" Check-In

©2016, Jacob Porter, Daring Ventures

Regular Communication to Rebuild Trust

Wounding Partner	Wounded Partner
Sobriety: "My sobriety date is....."	Safety: "My safety level today is...." (Provide a number between 0 and 10)
Accountability: "I want to apologize for when..."	Acknowledge: "I felt safest this week when..."
Feelings: "This week, the emotions I felt most were..."	Feelings: "This week, the emotions I felt most were..."
Express: "I've been learning about myself...."	Express: "I had the hardest time this week when..."
Recovery: "For my recovery, I have...and plan to..."	Requests: "You can help me feel safer by..."

HELPING MY PARTNER HEAL (PART 1)

Instructions for completing the SAFER Check-In:

1. Set a designated weekly time and place for the check-in. Try to choose a time when you will be uninterrupted and not too tired.
2. Plan ahead for check-in. Be prepared with what you are going to say. Preparation can greatly enhance the experience by making it more thoughtful and meaningful.
3. Decide whether the wounding or wounded partner will share first. The first person will share their complete check-in. Then the second person will share their complete check-in.
4. While each person shares their check-in, the other person should try to use good talking and listening boundaries if they respond.
5. Remember, this process involves 2 traumatized people being vulnerable. Be gentle with yourselves and take a break before you come back to discuss any content/concerns in detail.

Step 2 Connection: Make a choice today to believe that your relationship can be repaired. With the help of a higher power, all things are possible. With your partner, choose to believe, and ask for help with any unbelief you may have. In the space below, write a prayer about this desire to want to believe.

| |
| |

*** Close every day of daily check-in with your partner with prayer. If you need a helpful acronym to P.R.A.Y., then be sure to P = Praise the good, R = Respond to challenges, A = Ask for help, and Y = Yield to the will of your higher power

<u>**PARTNER CONNECT**</u> If you haven't done so already, talk with your partner and arrange a daily time that works for both of you to do the check in.

THE FOUNDATIONS OF RECOVERY - PART 1 GROUND ZERO

 **Exercise 41**   **Feeling Wheel**

"You got to Feel it to Heal it."

There are many exercises in this book that will require you to access where you or your partner lands on the wheel. We all fluctuate around the wheel throughout the day.

Treat this tool as a bullseye and apply it in two ways:

1. Identify your own feelings, starting in the middle-to-outer parts of the circle. Then, work toward the inward primary emotion. You can say something like:
   "I feel scared…really anxious about today."

2. Hear the feelings of others, namely your partner.
   First, they share what they are thinking or experiencing.
   Then, ask what feeling(s) are connected to that for them.
   Allow them space to get to the center of the wheel.

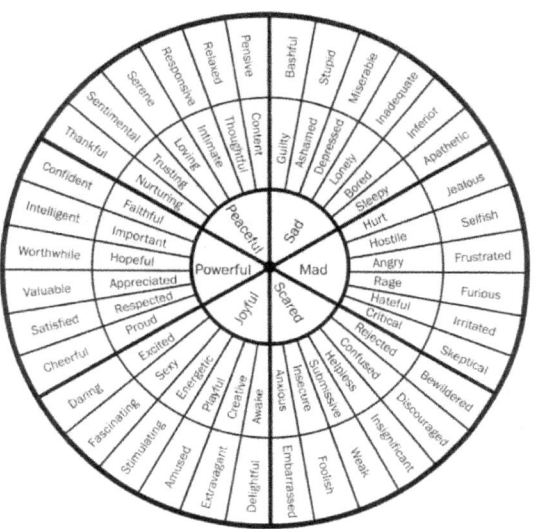

In your recovery from SA and/or IA, your ability to access your feelings can help identify what leads you into unhealthy thinking and/or lust.

See Appendix

In the next week, identify 2 feelings per day. Also, identify if you would have coped with these feelings with either sexual addiction or intimacy avoidant behavior.

Day	Feelings	Reason for feeling OR "I'd act out in _____ (SA/PA/IA) to cope"
1		
2		
3		
4		
5		
6		
7		

HELPING MY PARTNER HEAL (PART 1)

Step 3 Connection: Turning your will over to a higher power is a daily process. This involves letting go of your will and trusting in this power's will for your life. This is done with every feeling and desire of your heart. Write 3 statements of surrender for the feelings you recorded above.

> Ex: "I surrender this feeling of _____ to you. I ask that your will be done, not my own, and that you will reveal what it is I need to find in you, not in my fleshly destructive coping mechanisms."
> - 1.
> - 2.
> - 3.

PARTNER CONNECT For the next 30 days, ask your partner to identify a feeling from the Feelings Wheel that they are experiencing and share it with you. Listen to what they have to say. Ask them to share what they are experiencing that contributed to their feeling.

 **Exercise 42**   **Most Flawed Moment**

Sharing your daily flawed moments creates vulnerability and a deeper emotional connection with your partner.

We who are sexually addicted or intimacy avoidant put ourselves in the "good box" or "bad box." We think in black and white when it comes to being lovable, and while we all have flawed moments, the point of this exercise is to realize that you are still loveable even when you make a mistake.

Examples of what to share for Flawed Moments: Expressing anger towards a child or being defensive towards your partner

Examples of what to not to share for Flawed Moments: Driving over a curb or stubbing a toe

It's about getting vulnerable. We share the week's most flawed moment in recovery groups in order to experience acceptance even though we make mistakes.

Have your actions caused you to feel broken or ashamed? List specific ones here and share them with a sponsor or recovery partner.

If your partner is open to it, practice sharing your flawed moment accompanied with acceptance for a week.

	Day 1	Day 2	Day 3	Day 4	Day 5	Day 6	Day 7
Flawed Moment							

When your partner shares their flawed moment, respond with **"Thank you for telling me. I still love you."**

HELPING MY PARTNER HEAL (PART 1)

Step 2 Connection: Belief in a higher power means that we are fully known and accepted. Do you believe that about yourself? Why? If not, what characteristic(s) of your higher power opposes being known and accepted regardless of your flawed moments?

[   ]

PARTNER CONNECT Ask your partner if they are open to doing this exercise with you. If they are, practice it every day with them.

Maintain a Sobriety Focus

Staying Sober Checklist   Exercise 43

This exercise is specifically for the sexually addicted who need to reflect on their actions pertaining to a relapse from sobriety. Your addict mind will try to bend boundaries, make excuses, and lie (to name a few) in order to return to lust and fantasy. Space is provided for you to reflect on anything else related to your relapsing. The point of this exercise is to self-evaluate and get back into the game of recovery. You are worth it!

	Yes	No	What I Plan to Do About It?
I stopped wearing my rubber band			
I played the victim, not taking 100% responsibility for my recovery			
I haven't made daily recovery calls			
I used electronic devices with no accountability software or blockers on them			
I haven't done the daily connecting exercises with my partner 6/7 times in the week			
I was lying prior to breaking sobriety			
I avoided intimacy with my partner prior to breaking sobriety			
I have stopped engaging my partner with the weekly check-in			
I have been grooming or flirting			
I have been objectifying others			
I have had fantasy thoughts that I ruminate on without taking them captive and telling others in recovery			
I haven't done my gratitude's 6/7 times in the week			

I haven't been consistently doing Book Work			

Step 3 Connection: Return to placing your will and trust in your higher power. No matter what you plan to do, let it into your heart to give you the power and desire to choose recovery. Write a prayer highlighting this step with regards to your break of sobriety.

PARTNER CONNECT Share at least 2 areas that you have identified for improvement with your partner. What is your plan for change? What are you going to do to be accountable for making these changes?

MAINTAIN A SOBRIETY FOCUS

3 Circles

Exercise 44

The 3 circles represent the areas of recovery all our actions fall into.

Inner Circle:

These are the actions we consider as "acting out" in either sexual addiction or intimacy avoidance.

Middle Circle:

These are the situations, breaking of boundaries, or actions done that may lead to you acting out in your inner circle behavior. (Ex: see HALT BS exercise)

Outer Circle:

These are the healthy behaviors that you do on a day-to-day basis. Using recovery tools, engaging with your partner, and maintaining a healthy self all belong here.

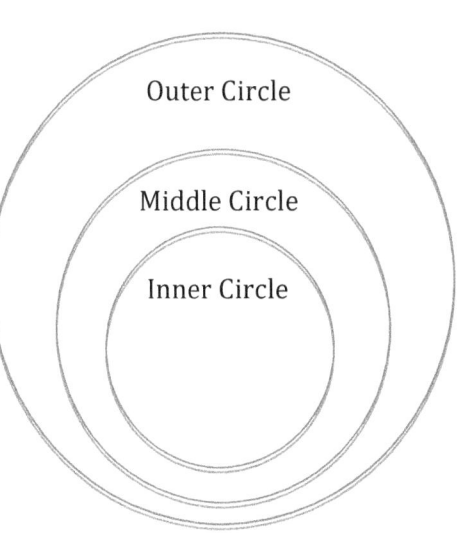

In the table below, identify 4 behaviors for each circle and the consequences of those actions for yourself and your partner. Consequences are how it affects or impacts you and your partner.

Inner Circle Behaviors	Consequences for Yourself	Consequences for Your Partner
1.		
2.		
3.		
4.		
Middle Circle Behaviors	**Consequences for Yourself**	**Consequences for Your Partner**
1.		
2.		
3.		
4.		
Outer Circle Behaviors	**Consequences for Yourself**	**Consequences for Your Partner**
1.		
2.		
3.		
4.		

THE FOUNDATIONS OF RECOVERY - PART 1 GROUND ZERO

Step 1 Connection: Share your behaviors and consequences with someone on a recovery call. You are not alone in this! We get better working with others in our recovery.

__PARTNER CONNECT__ Share your inner, middle, and outer circle behaviors with your partner.

SA/PA Lapse and Relapse Worksheet

Exercise 45

Here, we return to the underlying heart issues that can very easily send you back into your sexual addiction coping strategies. This is your story. Your mind will always have tattooed into it the images of fantasy and feelings, but they could never be satisfied. In completing this exercise, you will be able to tell the story of your broken heart and mind and how you can now be freed daily from it.

Instructions: Answer the following questions to help you figure out what led you to your Sexual Addiction (SA)/Pornography Addiction (PA) behavior.

Describe the main reason you used pornography or behaved in a sexually inappropriate way.

Describe the inner thoughts and feelings that triggered your need or desire to use pornography or act out sexually.

Describe any external circumstances that triggered your need or desire to use pornography or act out sexually.

Think back to when this started. Describe the first decision you made (or remember making) that started the lapse or relapse process.

Step 10 Connection: Recovery is ongoing. Name a step, from steps 1-9, that has been meaningful for your ongoing recovery from SA/PA and why.

___

PARTNER CONNECT If you have already confessed your SA and PA behavior to your partner, please share this exercise with them. Describe what you have learned about yourself.

Appreciation and Resignation Letters for SA/PA/Infidelity

Exercise 46

We begin this exercise by recognizing and appreciating what your sex addiction has provided for you. This is an important process of recovery because your perception of sex has been shaped by years of experiences. You resorted to acting out to soothe yourself, cope with life, feel powerful, feel loved, control satisfaction, be content, escape your circumstances, relive fantasy, and/or satiate your sexual desires.

Your connection to sex, whether acting out with others or yourself, has provided something for you. Recall those times when you held value for your sexual addiction. Even though it may have been momentary, what was the nature of appreciation you can name? Record at least 10.

1. _____
2. _____
3. _____
4. _____
5. _____
6. _____
7. _____
8. _____
9. _____
10. _____

Now, using these, write a letter to the sexual addiction as if it were a person standing in front of you, like a friend who has benefited you. Whether in your childhood or adulthood, the addiction gave you a sense of false control, happiness, satisfaction, and comfort.

Dear sex addiction,

Thank you for

_____
_____
_____
_____
_____
_____
_____
_____
_____

THE FOUNDATIONS OF RECOVERY - PART 1 GROUND ZERO

MAINTAIN A SOBRIETY FOCUS

Next, you will pair this appreciation with resignation.

Resignation will be necessary for you to move on from the destruction that sex addiction has caused you. Think of how that friend of addiction has lied to, stolen from, tricked, and misguided you. Recognize the pain, grief, damage, and destruction the addiction has caused you, your relationships, and your children. Look addiction in the eyes and choose to say goodbye. Resign from the fantasy and lies it has told you and choose to live in reality.

Think of at least 15 reasons to resign.

1. _____
2. _____
3. _____
4. _____
5. _____
6. _____
7. _____
8. _____
9. _____
10. _____
11. _____
12. _____
13. _____
14. _____
15. _____

Now, this time using these 15 or more points of hurt and/or destruction above, write a letter to the sexual addiction, formally divorcing yourself and your life from this addiction that has cost so much.

Dear sexual addiction,

I resign. It's time for you to go.

_____
_____
_____
_____
_____
_____
_____
_____
_____

THE FOUNDATIONS OF RECOVERY - PART 1 GROUND ZERO

Step 3 Connection: Ask your higher power for the will, the way, and the strength to face whatever comes, to cope with life the way it wants you to. Express a desperation and dependency upon its will for your life.

PARTNER CONNECT Do not share this activity with your partner. They are not likely to appreciate hearing how your addiction has benefitted you, even if this is a reality. Understand that your addiction has hurt them and their experience with your recovery is very different than yours.

MAINTAIN A SOBRIETY FOCUS

SA/PA Relapse Chain — Exercise 47

Instructions: The last link in the relapse chain represents your use of pornography or other sexually addicted behaviors. Each preceding link represents a specific relapse warning sign. Identify as many warning signs as you can. Then state how much time elapsed between the earliest warning sign and the first time you acted out again. Also, state how you felt about acting out, and how your partner felt.

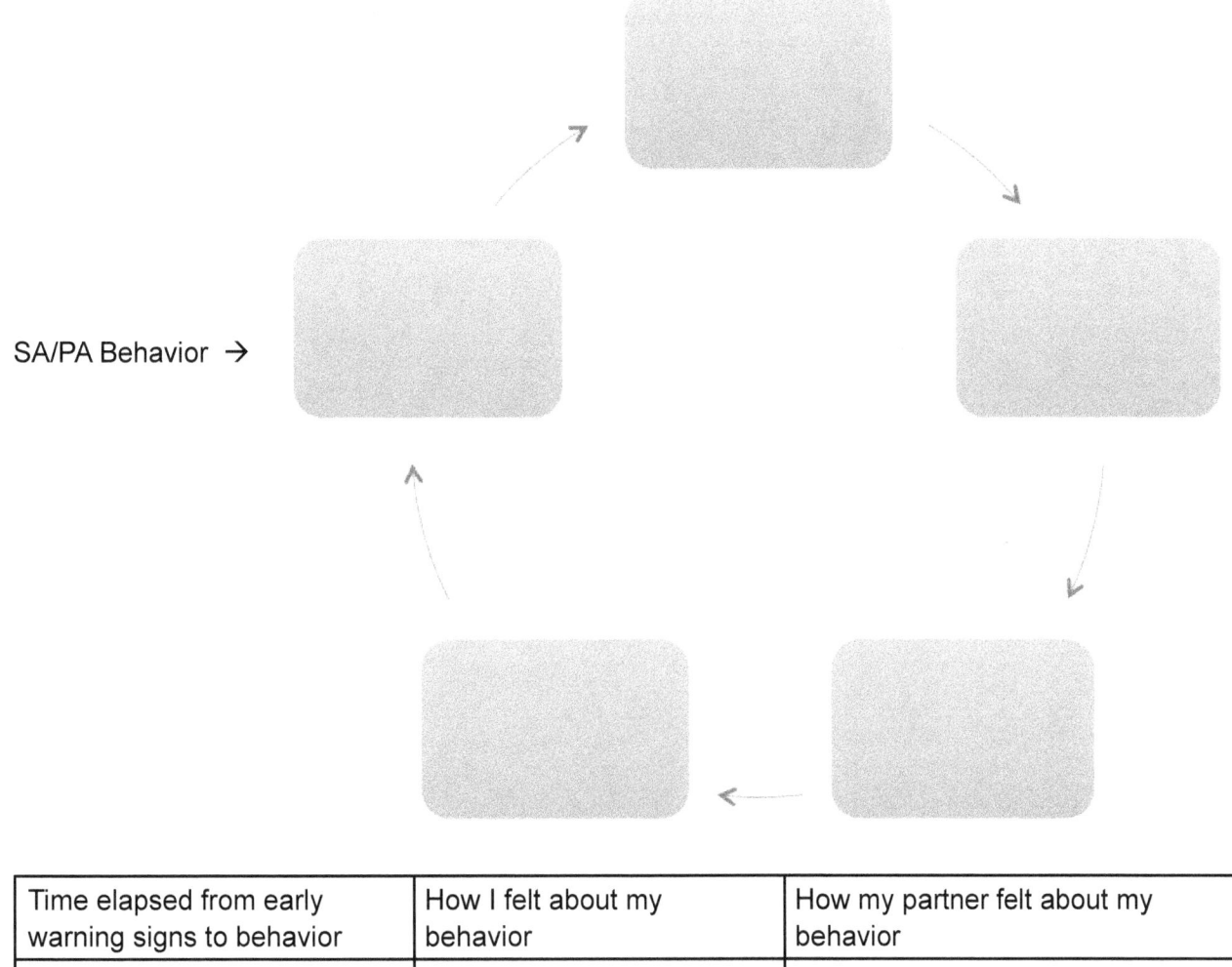

SA/PA Behavior →

Time elapsed from early warning signs to behavior	How I felt about my behavior	How my partner felt about my behavior

Step 1 Connection: Name the warning signs that you are powerless over. Then, name choices you use can manage or stop.

___

PARTNER CONNECT Please share with your partner the choices you identified as helpful in keeping you from relapsing.

SA/PA Relapse Prevention Plan   Exercise 48

Relapses can happen very quickly in isolation, and because of pride in your own effort and willpower. This is why it is so important to humble ourselves daily about our need to retrain our mind over time and to lean on one another for support. Below are lines to describe how you will prevent relapses, and consequences for yourself if you don't. Our lives are unmanageable in addiction. Make the necessary choices to heal and recover!

Coping Skills: List at least 3 activities or skills you can use to get your mind away from acting out sexually or using pornography.

1. _____
2. _____
3. _____

Social Support: List at least 3 people you can talk to who you know will give you the truth when you are thinking about acting out.

1. _____
2. _____
3. _____

Consequences: In the left-hand column, list 4 consequences to your life if you continue to act out. In the right-hand column, list 4 benefits to your life if you remain sober from sex and/or pornography addiction.

Relapse Outcomes	Sobriety Outcomes

THE FOUNDATIONS OF RECOVERY - PART 1 GROUND ZERO

In addition to your own consequences, list at least 3 ways that your relapse would negatively affect your partner. If you're having trouble, ask your partner.

1._____
2._____
3._____

Step 3 Connection: Express trust in your higher power for the strength and determination to obediently follow this plan. Sit in silence for 5 minutes, opening your heart to its will for your life. Reflect on the experience here.

[ ]

PARTNER CONNECT If you have already confessed your SA and PA behavior to your partner, please share this exercise with them. Describe what you have learned about yourself.

MAINTAIN A SOBRIETY FOCUS

Top 5 Intimacy Avoidance   Exercise 49

Out of the list of 40 intimacy avoidant behaviors or ways of thinking, mark your top 20 ways of avoidance in relationships. Then, have your partner mark their ideas of the top 20.

Lack of Empathy	Sexual Gratification Outside of Relationship	Easily Offended	Frequent Lying	Feelings are Facts	Emotionally Disengaged	Defensive	Sexually Avoidant
Self-Preoccupied	Constant Activity	Sabotages Emotional Connection	Blame-Shifting	Cynical Script	Poor Demeanor	All-or-Nothing Thinking	Avoid taking Responsibility
Stonewalling	Plays the Victim	Oversensitive to Criticism	Doing it My Way	Hero to Zero	Focuses on Faults of Others	Jumps to Conclusions	Contempt for Self/Others
Labels Themselves and Others	Requires Hoop Jumping	Prideful or Unteachable	Objectifies	Offends from a Victim Position	Suspicious of Partner	Reactive vs. Proactive in Relationship	Breadcrumbing or Love Bombing
Low Emotional Expression or Bandwidth	Inability to Handle Conflict Productively	Poor Self-Reflection	Gaslighting	Max or Min of Faults or Good Deeds	Spiritually Independent or Disengaged	Married but Unloved	An Intense Need to be Right

Now write out your top 10 based on these.

Lastly, with your partner, decide which 5 you will work on for the first 90 days and the second 90 days.

1st 90	2nd 90
1.	1.
2.	2.
3.	3.
4.	4.
5.	5.

THE FOUNDATIONS OF RECOVERY - PART 1 GROUND ZERO

Step 1 Connection: Recovery has choices. You will discover what you're powerless over and what you have the power to choose. Choose the date on a calendar, 180 days from now, when you will return to these top 10 and reassess, with your partner, which behaviors you are still showing.

I will revisit these top 10 with my partner on _____(Date 180 days from now)
Signature_____

<u>PARTNER CONNECT</u> Ask for your partner's input to help you create your list of IA behaviors.

Be sure to include your partner in all parts of this exercise. Share your commitment to revisit your top 10 with them. Remember, this is a contract between you and your partner. Failure to follow through on your part will hurt them more than they have already been hurt and will break their trust in your relationship.

Intimacy Avoidance – Appreciation and Resignation Letters

Exercise 50

Use the previous exercise - Top 5 IA

Express your appreciation and resignation to your ways of avoidant thinking and behaviors.

Go into detail about <u>what you gained</u> or <u>got out of acting the way you do</u>.

You will write 5 letters of appreciation and resignation, addressed to your behaviors.

Note: An extra appreciation and resignation page is provided for a sixth letter.

I write this to express **appreciation** for _____. (intimacy avoidant behavior #1)

_____
_____
_____
_____
_____
_____
_____
_____
_____
_____
_____
_____
_____
_____
_____
_____
_____
_____
_____
_____
_____
_____
_____

THE FOUNDATIONS OF RECOVERY - PART 1 GROUND ZERO

I write this to **resign** from acting _____. (intimacy avoidant behavior #1)

MAINTAIN A SOBRIETY FOCUS

I write this to express **appreciation** for _____. (intimacy avoidant behavior #2)

THE FOUNDATIONS OF RECOVERY - PART 1 GROUND ZERO

I write this to **resign** from acting _____. (intimacy avoidant behavior #2)

MAINTAIN A SOBRIETY FOCUS

I write this to express **appreciation** for _____. (intimacy avoidant behavior #3)

THE FOUNDATIONS OF RECOVERY - PART 1 GROUND ZERO

I write this to **resign** from acting _____. (intimacy avoidant behavior #3)

MAINTAIN A SOBRIETY FOCUS

I write this to express **appreciation** for _____. (intimacy avoidant behavior #4)

THE FOUNDATIONS OF RECOVERY - PART 1 GROUND ZERO

I write this to **resign** from acting _____. (intimacy avoidant behavior #4)

MAINTAIN A SOBRIETY FOCUS

I write this to express **appreciation** for _____. (intimacy avoidant behavior #5)

THE FOUNDATIONS OF RECOVERY - PART 1 GROUND ZERO

I write this to **resign** from acting _____. (intimacy avoidant behavior #5)

MAINTAIN A SOBRIETY FOCUS

I write this to express **appreciation** for _____. (intimacy avoidant behavior #6)

THE FOUNDATIONS OF RECOVERY - PART 1 GROUND ZERO

I write this to **resign** from acting _____. (intimacy avoidant behavior #6)

___

PARTNER CONNECT Do not share this activity with your partner. They are not likely to appreciate hearing how your IA has benefitted you, even if this is a reality. Understand that your behavior has deeply hurt them, and their experience with your recovery is very different than yours.

MAINTAIN A SOBRIETY FOCUS

IA Relapse Chain

Exercise 51

The last link in the relapse chain represents your use of IA behaviors. Each preceding link represents a specific relapse warning sign. Identify as many warning signs as you can. Then state how much time elapsed between the earliest warning sign and the first time you acted in an IA behavior again. Also, state how you felt about acting IA, and how your partner felt.

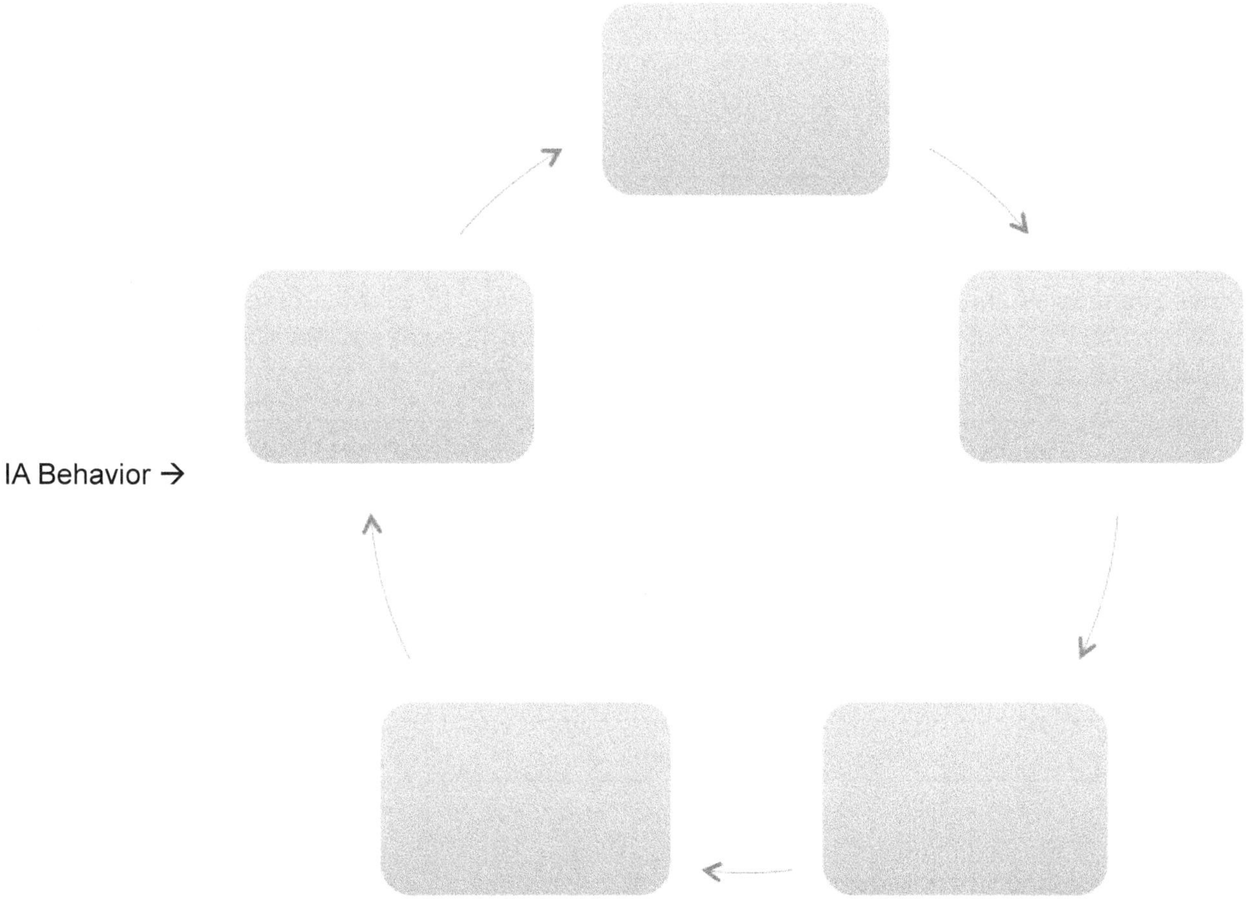

IA Behavior →

Time elapsed from early warning signs to behavior	How I felt about my behavior	How my partner felt about my behavior

Step 1 Connection: Name the warning signs that you are powerless over. Then, name choices you must use to manage your warning signs to cease from causing others pain with your avoidant behaviors.

<u>**PARTNER CONNECT**</u> Share what you wrote in Step 1 with your partner. What are the warning signs you have identified? What are the choices you can make to get yourself out of the relapse cycle?

Exercise 52   IA Relapse Prevention Plan

Coping Skills: List at least 3 activities or skills you can use to get your mind away from behaving in avoidant ways.

1. _____
2. _____
3. _____

Social Support: List at least 3 people you can talk to who you know will give you the truth when you're thinking about avoiding your partner or any relationship.

1. _____
2. _____
3. _____

Consequences: In the left-hand column, list 4 consequences to your life if you continue to avoid intimate emotional relationships. In the right-hand column, list 4 benefits to your life if you are engaging in healthy mindsets and engaging in your closest relationships.

Relapse Outcomes	Relational Outcomes

In addition to your own consequences, list at least 3 ways that your relapse into avoidant behaviors would negatively affect your partner. If you're having trouble, ask your partner how they feel and why.

1. _____
2. _____
3. _____

Step 3 Connection: Express trust in your higher power for the strength and determination to obediently follow this plan. Sit in silence with him for 5 minutes, opening your heart to its will for your life. Name each of your intimacy avoidant behaviors during your silence. Reflect on the experience here.

PARTNER CONNECT Share this activity in its entirety with your partner. Ask them if they can identify anything you have missed.

Parting Words

In closing, I would like to thank you for using this workbook. We hope that it was helpful to you. While I know the road is long and tough to navigate, I encourage you to keep pressing on. As Winston Churchill once said, "If you are going through hell, keep going." If you do the work, don't give in, and seek help along the way, I know you will find your way out of the painful circumstances in which you have found yourself. We wish you healing, comfort, peace, and wholeness in your recovery journey.

Addendum

Yearly Tracker

Use this tracker combined with the weekly check-in to keep track of your efforts in recovery for the next year

Month	Dr/ N/R	Present in Relationship	Rating of Relationship	# of Calls	Recovery Score /100	Month	Dr/ N/R	Present in Relationship	Rating of Relationship	# of Calls	Recovery Score /100
Jan	/ /	/ 10	/ 10		/ 100	July	/ /	/ 10	/ 10		/ 100
	/ /	/ 10	/ 10		/ 100		/ /	/ 10	/ 10		/ 100
	/ /	/ 10	/ 10		/ 100		/ /	/ 10	/ 10		/ 100
	/ /	/ 10	/ 10		/ 100		/ /	/ 10	/ 10		/ 100
	/ /	/ 10	/ 10		/ 100		/ /	/ 10	/ 10		/ 100
Feb	/ /	/ 10	/ 10		/ 100	Aug	/ /	/ 10	/ 10		/ 100
	/ /	/ 10	/ 10		/ 100		/ /	/ 10	/ 10		/ 100
	/ /	/ 10	/ 10		/ 100		/ /	/ 10	/ 10		/ 100
	/ /	/ 10	/ 10		/ 100		/ /	/ 10	/ 10		/ 100
	/ /	/ 10	/ 10		/ 100		/ /	/ 10	/ 10		/ 100
March	/ /	/ 10	/ 10		/ 100	Sept	/ /	/ 10	/ 10		/ 100
	/ /	/ 10	/ 10		/ 100		/ /	/ 10	/ 10		/ 100
	/ /	/ 10	/ 10		/ 100		/ /	/ 10	/ 10		/ 100
	/ /	/ 10	/ 10		/ 100		/ /	/ 10	/ 10		/ 100
	/ /	/ 10	/ 10		/ 100		/ /	/ 10	/ 10		/ 100
April	/ /	/ 10	/ 10		/ 100	Oct	/ /	/ 10	/ 10		/ 100
	/ /	/ 10	/ 10		/ 100		/ /	/ 10	/ 10		/ 100
	/ /	/ 10	/ 10		/ 100		/ /	/ 10	/ 10		/ 100
	/ /	/ 10	/ 10		/ 100		/ /	/ 10	/ 10		/ 100
	/ /	/ 10	/ 10		/ 100		/ /	/ 10	/ 10		/ 100
May	/ /	/ 10	/ 10		/ 100	Nov	/ /	/ 10	/ 10		/ 100
	/ /	/ 10	/ 10		/ 100		/ /	/ 10	/ 10		/ 100
	/ /	/ 10	/ 10		/ 100		/ /	/ 10	/ 10		/ 100
	/ /	/ 10	/ 10		/ 100		/ /	/ 10	/ 10		/ 100
	/ /	/ 10	/ 10		/ 100		/ /	/ 10	/ 10		/ 100
June	/ /	/ 10	/ 10		/ 100	Dec	/ /	/ 10	/ 10		/ 100
	/ /	/ 10	/ 10		/ 100		/ /	/ 10	/ 10		/ 100
	/ /	/ 10	/ 10		/ 100		/ /	/ 10	/ 10		/ 100
	/ /	/ 10	/ 10		/ 100		/ /	/ 10	/ 10		/ 100
	/ /	/ 10	/ 10		/ 100		/ /	/ 10	/ 10		/ 100

Feeling Wheel

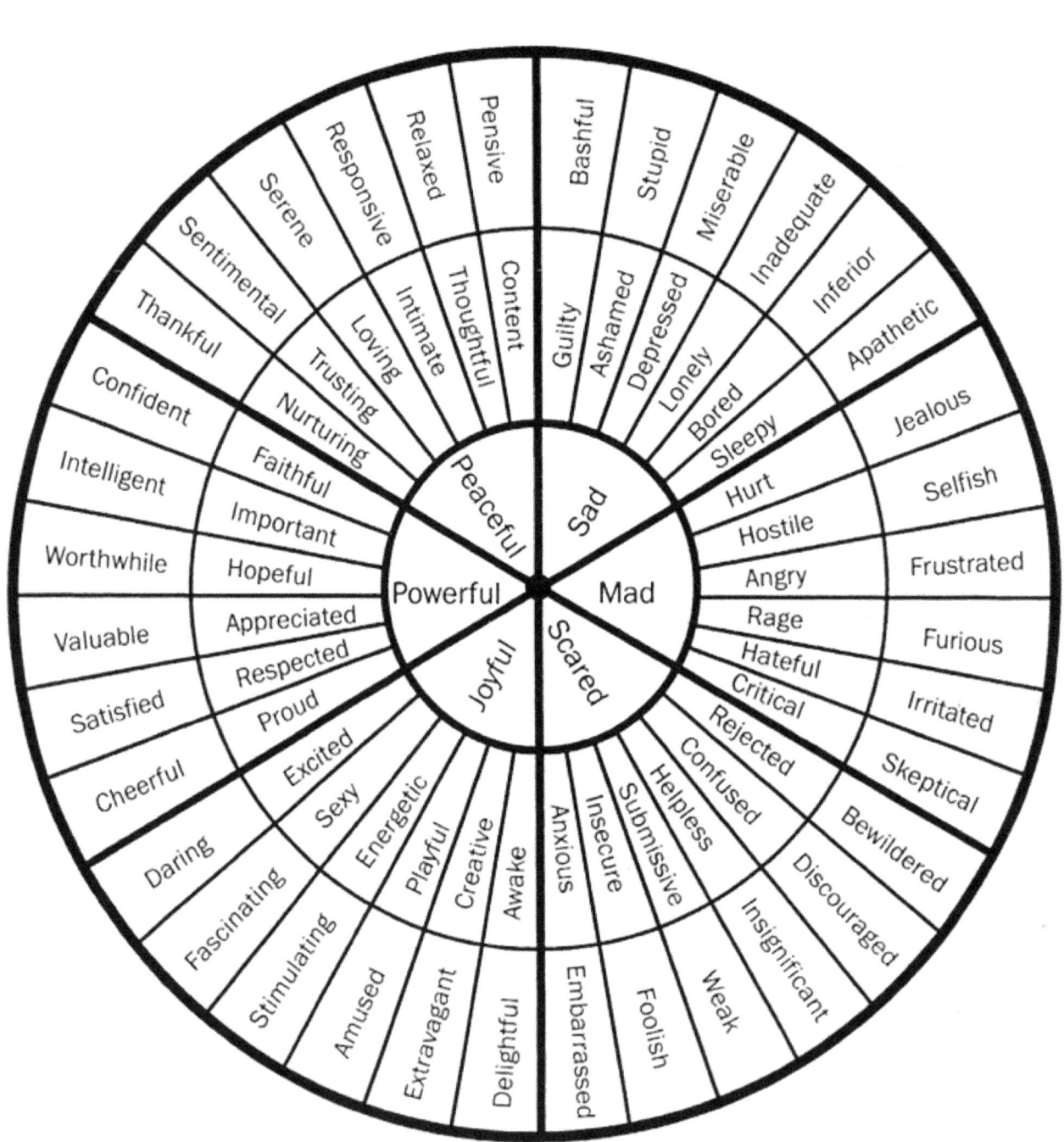

The Twelve Steps for Sexual Addiction

 **1** We admitted we were powerless over lust and that our lives had become unmanageable

 **2** We came to believe that a power greater than ourselves could restore us to sanity.

 **3** We made a decision to turn our will and lives over to the care of our higher power as we understand them.

 **4** We made a searching and fearless moral inventory of ourselves.

 **5** We admitted to our higher power, to ourselves, and to others the exact nature of our wrongs.

 **6** We were entirely ready to have our higher power remove all these defects of character.

 **7** We humbly asked our higher power to remove our struggle.

 **8** We made a list of all people we had harmed, and we became willing to make amends with them all.

 **9** We made direct amends to whomever possible, except when to do so would injure them or others.

 **10** We continue to take personal inventory and, when in the wrong, we promptly admit it.

 **11** We seek through prayer and meditation to improve contact with our higher power, praying for knowledge of their will for our lives and the strength to carry it out.

 **12** Having had a spiritual awakening from our experience through the steps, we seek to share with others and practice our principles in all our relationships.

The Twelve Steps for Intimacy Avoidance

 **1** We admitted we were powerless over avoidance and that our lives had become unmanageable

 **2** We came to believe that a power greater than ourselves could restore us to sanity.

 **3** We made a decision to turn our will and lives over to the care of our higher power as we understand them.

 **4** We made a searching and fearless moral inventory of ourselves.

 **5** We admitted to our higher power, to ourselves, and to others the exact nature of our wrongs.

 **6** We were entirely ready to have our higher power remove all these defects of character.

 **7** We humbly asked our higher power to remove our struggle.

 **8** We made a list of all people we had harmed, and we became willing to make amends with them all.

 **9** We made direct amends to whomever possible, except when to do so would injure them or others.

 **10** We continue to take personal inventory and, when in the wrong, we promptly admit it.

 **11** We seek through prayer and meditation to improve contact with our higher power, praying for knowledge of their will for our lives and the strength to carry it out.

 **12** Having had a spiritual awakening from our experience through the steps, we seek to share with others and practice our principles in all our relationships.

Recovery and 12 Step Prayers

Third Step Prayer (Page 63, AA Big Book)

God, I offer myself to Thee — to build with me and to do with me as Thou wilt. Relieve me of the bondage of self, that I may better do Thy will. Take away my difficulties, that victory over them may bear witness to those I would help of Thy Power, Thy Love, and Thy Way of life. May I do Thy will always!

Fourth Step Prayer (Page 67, AA Big Book)

This is a sick man. How can I be helpful to him? God, save me from being angry. Thy will be done.

Seventh Step Prayer (Page 76, AA Big Book)

My Creator, I am now willing that you should have all of me, good & bad. I pray that you now remove from me every single defect of character that stands in the way of my usefulness to you & my fellows. Grant me strength, as I go from here to do Your bidding. Amen.

Eighth Step Prayer (Page 76, AA Big Book)

Faith without works is dead.

Tenth Step Prayer (Page 85, AA Big Book)

How can I serve Thee? Thy will (not mine) be done.

Eleventh Step Prayer (Twelve Steps and Twelve Traditions, p. 99)

Lord, make me a channel of Thy peace – that where there is hatred, I may bring love – that where there is wrong, I may bring the spirit of forgiveness – that where there is discord, I may bring harmony – that where there is error, I may bring truth--that where there is doubt, I may bring faith--that where there is despair, I may bring hope – that where there are shadows, I may bring light – that where there is sadness, I may bring joy. Lord, grant that I may seek to comfort rather than to be comforted – to understand, than to be understood – to love, than to be loved. For it is by self-forgetting that one finds. It is by forgiving that one is forgiven. It is by dying that one awakens to eternal life. Amen

Serenity Prayer (Reinhold Niebuhr)

God, grant me the serenity to accept the things I cannot change,
The courage to change the things I can,
And the wisdom to know the difference.

40 ways to be IA
(Intimacy Avoidant)

1. **Marked lack of empathy.** Has trouble putting themselves in someone else's shoes. Often comes off as insensitive or uncaring. When others try to share their perspective, they often impose their own views on the situation without listening to the other person's view. Often has trouble understanding cause and effect - in other words, how their actions are contributing to the reactions of others.

2. **Oversensitivity to criticism or perceives criticism when there is none.** This may stem from a fear of rejection, poor self-esteem, or a generally negative view of others' intentions. Oversensitivity to criticism has been linked to negative childhood experiences such as harsh criticism from a parent or caregiver, rejection from peers, or having a parent with unrealistically high expectations. People who are oversensitive to criticism (real or perceived) often have negative cognitive biases that cause them to interpret information in a negative way.

3. **Low emotional expression and bandwidth.** Has an inability or unwillingness (oftentimes both) to express emotion. Emotional range is generally very small (2 or 3 emotions shared, usually some type of anger). The term "emotional bandwidth" refers to someone's ability to handle or engage in emotional stimuli, whether the stimulus is their own or someone else's.

4. **Jumps to conclusions.** Involves jumping to conclusions without having supporting facts. Mind-reading is when people randomly conclude that others are reacting negatively to them. Fortune-telling is assuming things are going to turn out badly and acting like those assumptions are already established facts.

5. **Contempt for self/others.** Contempt for self often comes across as shame and/or self-pity. Contempt for others comes out as grandiosity, belittling, or criticism.

6. **Sabotages emotional connectedness.** According to research studies, people who sabotage their relationships often have low self-esteem, difficulty trusting people (especially their partners), and a fear of commitment or being hurt, abandoned, or rejected.

7. **Reactive vs. Proactive in relationships.** This person appears ambivalent or disinterested in creating opportunities for ongoing, consistent connectedness. Major efforts to show love to their partner only come when the partner is fed up and entertaining the thought of ending the relationship. These efforts often fade away once the partner is reconnected to them, leading to an ongoing cycle that alternates between disinterest, emotional pain, and love-bombing.

8. **Spiritually independent or disengaged.** This person refuses to share any intimate details of their spirituality with their partner, often claiming that their spirituality is "private".

9. **Hoop jumping.** Often a feature of Intimacy Avoidant relationships, the IA will make their partner jump through a series of "hoops" to receive love. Much of this behavior is born out of entitlement. IAs often use this behavior as an excuse to withhold intimacy from their partner or criticize them for a "lack of performance."

10. **Defensiveness.** Defensive people often have issues of power and control. They often perceive confrontation and/or accountability as threats. The purpose of defensiveness is typically to protect a person from feeling hurt or shame. Defensiveness comes in many forms, including blame-shifting, silence, denial, and even self-pity.

11. **Prideful and/or Unteachable.** Typically, a person is masking feelings of low self-esteem and self-worth with pride. Pride is often a byproduct of feelings of inadequacy and vulnerability. Being "unteachable" can stem from pride, jealousy, stress, anxiety, or feelings of inadequacy.

12. **Blame-shifting.** People who blame-shift are often in denial about their level of personal responsibility. They often can't accept the fact that they may be at least partially responsible for a failure or mistake. Another reason for blame-shifting is to make the other person feel guilty or shamed, to silence them.

13. **Offended from victim position.** This takes place when a person decides that their role as victim gives them the right to lash out and/or hurt others. Pia Mellody and Terrence Real call this "retaliation." Intimacy Avoidant people often put themselves in the victim position through blame-shifting, shame, and self-pity. This makes it easier to justify bad behavior.
14. **Suspicious of partner.** There are many reasons IAs are suspicious of their partners. Common reasons include adverse childhood experiences that cause a general lack of trust toward others, depression and anxiety, and negative experiences in past relationships.
15. **Gaslighting.** Gaslighting is defined as psychological manipulation, typically over a prolonged period, that causes the victim to question their thoughts, feelings, memories, and perception of reality. Gaslighting typically involves lying but is not the same as lying. People often lie to escape consequences. Gaslighters lie to intentionally cause someone else to doubt themselves.
16. **Stonewalling/Punishing through anger.** Uses anger or silence to control the conversation. With silence, the partner eventually gives up, which is the intent. Anger is often used to intimidate, and punishing through anger is done purposely to teach the person a lesson and make them think twice about saying anything again. In either case, both are being used to silence someone.
17. **Frequent lying.** For IAs, lying often comes in the form of leaving out important information to avoid unwanted consequences. In some cases, habitual lying can be a sign of a more serious personality disorder.
18. **Avoids taking responsibility for actions.** This can be a result of emotional immaturity, denial, a refusal to be vulnerable, or an avoidance of intense feelings of remorse, guilt, and/or shame. In more serious cases, it can be because the person truly feels that accepting consequences is beneath them or does not have any understanding that their actions have consequences.
19. **Breadcrumbing or Love Bombing.** Breadcrumbing is a form of manipulation in which a person gives another person just enough attention and/or love to string them along. Love bombing often comes in the form of excessive flattery, attention, or gifts being used to lure someone to gain security for themselves.
20. **Emotionally disengaged.** This often stems from a deep fear of being ridiculed or rejected. An emotionally disengaged person may have learned from previous relationships that showing emotions made them vulnerable to negative consequences. Emotional disengagement is often developed in the family of origin when one or both parents failed to communicate their emotions or were uncomfortable with the emotions of others.
21. **Feelings are facts.** A person who treats feelings as facts often experiences emotions so intensely that they feel real. This typically stems from emotional immaturity. It's related to the cognitive distortion of emotional reasoning: "I feel it, so it must be true."
22. **Poor self-reflection.** Otherwise known as a lack of self-awareness. People with poor self-reflection are often intensely afraid of judgement and rejection from others. They keep themselves in a "protective bubble." This "bubble" makes it difficult for them to get in touch with their inner selves.
23. **Self-preoccupation.** This often stems from early childhood experiences of feeling rejected by others. They also could have been brought up to believe that they didn't have to consider the feelings of others. Trauma can also play a role because the person may have learned that they couldn't trust others, and this developed into self-preoccupation. Self-preoccupied people are generally emotionally immature.
24. **Labels themselves and others.** Related to the cognitive distortion of Labeling, which is a form of overgeneralization. It can also be related to perfectionism. For example, instead of being able to accept that they made a mistake, a person might label themselves a "loser." Instead of being understanding about the faults of others, they may label others "losers" or "idiots." Instead

of describing a situation realistically, labeling typically involves using inflammatory terms and language.

25. **Focuses on the faults of others.** Typically used as a defense mechanism in order to avoid feelings of guilt, shame, or inadequacy. It can also stem from entitlement when a person feels everyone else it at fault for them not getting what they want or feel they deserve.

26. **Objectification.** Treats their partner, others, and even themselves as objects. This extends far past sexual objectification or reducing someone to the sum of their body parts. Objectification also shows up as treating someone as if there is no need to be concerned about their experiences and/or feelings, a refusal to honor boundaries, treating people as if they were tools to be used for the IA to achieve their own goals, and treating someone as if they were easily replaced with someone else (a refusal to acknowledge someone's uniqueness).

27. **Poor demeanor.** Acts frequently disgruntled, angry, or irritated. Doesn't listen to their partner's feelings or discounts their experience. When asked to participate in the nurturing of the relationship, acts like it's a huge imposition. When asked to be accountable for past and/or present actions, responds with anger, blame, or pouting.

28. **Sexually disconnected or avoidant.** Doesn't make eye contact during sex or is mentally "checked out." Sex often feels empty and transactional to the partner. Also common is a complete/almost complete avoidance of sex. Couples that have sex 6 or fewer times per year are considered to have a "sexless" relationship.

29. **Sexual gratification outside of committed relationship.** This isn't always the case, but when it is it's typically due to an inability to connect with the partner. For most, this will be done through pornography and masturbation. For some, it will involve getting emotionally or sexually connected with a real person who is not their partner. Sexual addiction and attachment disorders are often underlying issues, especially with serial cheating.

30. **Inability to handle conflict productively.** For some, this will show up as conflict avoidance, stonewalling, and/or people-pleasing. For others, this will involve blame-shifting, denial, and overall defensiveness.

31. **All-or-nothing thinking (black-and-white thinking).** Seeing things in black and white without shades of gray. Tends to associate others and self into 2 categories: good and bad. Signs of all-or-nothing thinking include a tendency to use extreme terms when describing things, perfectionism, inability to see both good and bad in people and/or self, negative self-talk, and fear of trying new things.

32. **An intense need to be right.** Possible reasons for always needing to be right include insecurity, a need for control, a fear of failure, a competitive nature, and cognitive biases or distortions (such as all-or-nothing thinking) that make it difficult to consider alternate perspectives or admit it when wrong.

33. **Easily offended.** Often related to the cognitive distortion of personalization, which is assigning blame to oneself for circumstances out of one's control. Other reasons include unresolved psychological or emotional issues, a perception that their honor or personally held beliefs are being attacked, a generally negative emotional state, or the struggle to consider another's point of view.

34. **Maximization and minimization of faults and/or good deeds.** Tends to see others' faults as "huge" and their own as "not so bad." Tends to see their contributions as "huge" and others' contributions as minimal. In extreme cases, this can be due to grandiosity that contributes to a false sense of self-importance.

35. **Workaholism.** Many workaholics seek approval and become overly focused on work and "busyness" to gain approval and respect from others. Sometimes workaholism also occurs when the person is trying to avoid intimacy in their relationships.
36. **Plays the victim.** Playing the victim is a manipulative tactic. It is often used to avoid taking responsibility, gain sympathy and attention from others, and/or to discredit the experience and feelings of a person they have wronged.
37. **Hero or Zero.** Since IAs tend to see things in black and white without shades of gray, they tend to see themselves as a complete "hero" without faults or a "zero" with nothing but faults. This mentality often leads to blame-shifting, going "victim," and even complete denial of the issues.
38. **I did it my way.** This is an unwillingness to accept influence from their partner. IAs are typically highly independent and often don't listen to the suggestions of their partners when making decisions. Many partners define an IA partner as "an island."
39. **Cynical Script.** A bad story being played repeatedly in the person's head to excuse their poor treatment of the partner. The cynical script is often used to play the victim.
40. **Married but Unloved:** If married, the partner feels as if they are alone in it all. Many partners married to Intimacy Avoidants describe this as a surprise. It is common for Intimacy Avoidants to act differently before marriage than after marriage. Once the commitment to marriage is made, Intimacy Avoidants start to pull away from their partners in the ways that matter most. Partners may describe the relationship as sexless, devoid of intimacy, and disconnected.

Workgroups and Intensives

Men's Becoming Well Workgroups

Some guys have been in groups before; others have not. If you're committed to recovery from Sexual Addiction, Intimacy Avoidance, or Infidelity and are committed to rebuilding trust in your marriage, then our Men's Becoming Well Workgroups will be a good fit for you. Our men's groups focus on building and maintaining integrity, restoring intimacy in relationships, and rebuilding trust. They concentrate on two things: how to stop acting out and be accountable for the behavior that is breaking trust in the relationship, and how to develop the character and empathy it will take to support the relationship moving forward. And unlike many recovery groups out there, our guys are both finding sobriety and maintaining it.

Our groups are led by trained facilitators who have walked through many of these issues themselves, know how to stay sober, and know how to win in their relationship. The groups are small in size (no more than 8 people) so that each person can get the attention they need to address specific issues.

Each week, participants will hear a teaching from a trained professional and receive assignments and exercises that facilitate recovery for both themselves and their relationships. Participants will also have access to an online education portal, videos that explain the concepts talked about during group, and tutorials on how to work exercises and complete assignments.

Another thing that makes our groups different is that we welcome input from the wounded partners. Most programs exclude the partner, expecting that they stay in a relationship and take their partner's word for it that they're doing the work. When we hear from partners about past experiences, they often complain that nothing was shared with them, and they didn't even know what was going on most of the time.

Although we want to stress that the men need to own and work through their own recovery, and no partner can do that for them, we assign exercises to include the partner in rebuilding the relationship. Additionally, we offer a free monthly video conference call in which we update partners on what the guys will be working on that month and allow them to ask questions. Those meetings are typically led by Matt and Laura Burton personally.

Join a Men's Becoming Well workgroup today
www.BecomingWellInstitute.com

Men's Sexual Addiction, Infidelity & Intimacy Avoidance Recovery Intensives

Sexual addiction, infidelity, and intimacy avoidance can be isolating. Whether they're recovering from physical or emotional affairs, infidelity through pornography or other forms of sexual acting out, or intimacy avoidance, men entering recovery often feel like they are going it alone. Maximize your intensive experience by joining with other men to work through issues common to sexual addiction, infidelity, and intimacy avoidance. A Men's 3-Day Recovery Intensive can provide you with a safe environment to voice your pain and concerns, and to learn techniques for healing.

Intensives in a group format provide hope that you are not alone. You will hear the stories and struggles of others. You will also hear from Laura Burton, a trained and certified coach and a partner of someone who struggled with intimacy avoidance and pornography addiction. This will allow you to gain a deeper understanding of what both you and your partner are experiencing during this tough time in your relationship. You will not only see things through your relationship's historical lens, but through the eyes of others. This can help you gain a much-needed perspective that will help you move forward in recovery. Intensives focus on breaking the hold that addiction, infidelity, and intimacy avoidance have had on you and your partner. We partner with you to solve the issues that are holding you back from having the connection you have always wanted.

The Men's 3-Day Recovery Intensive offers daily group meetings and instruction by experts to ensure that the experience is tailored to you. Contact us today to schedule your intensive. Even if you are not currently in a relationship, the perspective you will gain throughout the intensive will help prepare you for the future—however that may look.

- Intensives are limited to 14 men per session.
- They take place at the Becoming Well Institute Intensive Center in sunny Tucson, Arizona.
- This includes an intake and assessment to identify your specific needs.
- We currently offer 2 distinct intensives for men: one with a focus on intimacy avoidance and one with a focus on sexual addiction and sexual/emotional infidelity.
- Each intensive is comprised of a combination of workgroups, group education, homework, exercises to work on with your partner, and personalized recovery plans.
- Contact us for pricing.

Our intensive center is located in beautiful, sunny Tucson, Arizona.

Learn more or sign up for a Men's Recovery Intensive today
www.BecomingWellInstitute.com

Sober Is Not Well
Men's "Going Deeper" Healing Intensives

Are you working on your recovery from porn/sexual addiction and intimacy avoidance? If so, why is your marriage still struggling so much and why do you still have behaviors and/or belief systems that are stunting you and your marriage from truly becoming well?

Why are you still stuck? Why aren't you getting a lot better? Why isn't your marriage getting a lot better? Because Sober is not Well. The areas underlying the SA and IA must be addressed. It's time to take another step in your recovery journey and focus on the roots.

In the Men's "Going Deeper" Healing Intensive, you'll focus on 4 specific areas of the 16 roots that slow or block recovery. These areas will be identified through a 2-part assessment process, one with you and the other getting your partner's input. You will spend your intensive time focused on the 4 identified focus areas in a process we call "Depth Work." That work will happen throughout the 3 ½-day intensive. The 16 root areas of potential intensive focus are:

Past Hurts Focus: Healing the injuries of your past to lessen their impact on you today and in the future.

o Trauma Focus; o Loss Focus; o Neglect Focus; o Abandonment Focus

Adaptive Behaviors Focus: Dismantling recurring struggles that are destroying you and/or your marriage and have you stuck.

o Other Addictions/Addiction Swapping Focus; o Anger Focus; o Specific Avoidance Focus; o Sexless Marriage Focus (Relational Sexual Avoidance); o Shame Focus; o Chronic Lying Focus; o Low or Lack of Empathy Focus; o Over Controlling of Self & Others' Focus; o Narcissistic Characteristics Focus; o Perpetual Victim Focus; o Emotional Immaturity Focus; o Chronic Negative Thinking Focus

The Details:

- Men's Healing Intensives are limited to 14 men per week.
- Healing Intensives take place on Thursday-Sunday.
- Your intensive will include intake assessment sessions to identify your particular needs.
- Each intensive weekend is comprised of groups, learning, processing, specific exercises, and personalized recovery plans.
- The time commitment per day is approximately 8 hours.
- Healing Intensive weekends are offered in-person only.

Our intensive center is located in beautiful, sunny Tucson, Arizona.
www.BecomingWellInstitute.com

Couple's Group Intensives
Moving couples from "Shattered to Strong"

Sexual addiction, infidelity, and intimacy avoidance can be isolating. Couples entering recovery often feel like they are going through it alone. Maximize your intensive experience by joining with other couples to work through issues common to infidelity and intimacy avoidance. A Couple's Group Intensive can provide you with a safe environment to voice your pain, concerns, and learn techniques for healing. Often, couples working through infidelity feel alone, judged, and hopeless. Intensives in a group format provide hope that you are not alone. You will hear the stories and struggles of others. This will allow you to gain a deeper understanding of what you and your partner are going through during this crisis. You will not only see things through your relationship's historical lens but also through the eyes of others. This can help you gain a much-needed perspective that will move you forward in recovery.

Group Intensive Weekends offer daily group meetings, instruction by experts, and individual sessions to help ensure that your experience is tailor-made for you. Couples leave feeling validated, understood, and hopeful— even if they were initially nervous about sharing their experience with others. Group Intensive Weekends will allow you to make connections with other people who understand what you are going through. This makes it possible for you to receive ongoing support through the relationships you form over the weekend. Couples will leave the Intensive with three distinct recovery plans: one for the wounding partner, one for the wounded partner, and one for the relationship.

- For couples who are in crisis after the recent discovery or disclosure of infidelity.
- For couples who are stuck and don't know how to get better.
- For couples who have experienced the isolation of infidelity, addiction, and intimacy avoidance and want to join a community of people who understand.
- For couples who want to learn from the experience of others in a safe environment.
- For couples who have done recovery work and want to deepen their experience.
- For couples who need a safe space to deal with what happened without feeling judged.
- For couples who want to hear from experts on how to recover from infidelity.
- For couples who want to accomplish in 3 days what normally takes 4-6 months.

The Details:

- Group Intensives take place in person on Thursday, Friday, and Saturday.
- Group Intensive Weekends include intake and assessment sessions to identify your specific needs.
- Each Group Intensive Weekend is comprised of a combination of workgroups, learning, homework, couple-specific exercises, and personalized recovery plans.
- The time commitment per day for Intensive Weekends is approximately 8-10 hours.

Learn more or sign up for a Couple's Group Intensive today
www.BecomingWellInstitute.com

Couples 7-Day: All In One Group Intensives

Are you a guy or married to a guy who's stuck or in a downward spiral, relationally or in your individual recovery, and who's unable to do what's needed/necessary to heal the shattered trust in your relationship?

What if you could experience all 4 intensives that Becoming Well Institute offers in a week? This means he could get the help he needs for his addiction and/or avoidance, as well as begin to heal the roots that created them. At the same time, she could begin to heal from a broken heart and shattered trust. You, as a couple, could begin to repair what has to date seemed impossible to heal.

Well, you can do all this through our 7-day All-In-One Intensive. At this intensive, the woman does key segments of the Women's Wounded Partner Intensive with other women also attending. The man does key segments of the Men's Recovery Intensive and Men's Going Even Deeper Intensive with the other men. Both partners work through key segments of the Couples Group intensive together, with the focus on helping couples navigate SA and IA recovery and Rebuilding Trust.

The four intensives that this all-in-one draws from:

- The Men's Recovery Intensive is for men striving to find lasting sobriety from porn addiction, sexual addiction, physical infidelity, emotional infidelity, intimacy avoidance, and/or sexual avoidance.
- The Wounded Partners Healing Intensive is for partners impacted by their wounding partner's sexual betrayal, intimacy avoidance, and/or sexual avoidance behaviors.
- The Men's "Going Deeper" Healing Intensives focus on the roots that created the addictive and destructive behaviors.
- The Couples Group Intensive helps couples understand what couple recovery looks like and what it takes to repair and rebuild the relationship, especially in the area of trust. It creates clarity and understanding of whether the wounding partner is serious about recovery and what the wounded partner should expect. It also creates a deeper understanding of what the benchmarks and timelines are for healing, all while supplying the tools and practice necessary to increase the likelihood for success.
- BONUS: Our All-In-One Intensive also teaches you how to help your School-Age and Adult Children Heal from the impacts of SA and IA.

For less than half of the total combined cost of all four intensives, you can experience them all. More importantly, you both benefit from the increased recovery & healing each intensive brings.

This is a great option for anyone wanting to accelerate the healing process, because intensives condense 4-6 months' worth of session work into 7 days.

Learn more or sign up for a Guys Group Intensive today
www.BecomingWellInstitute.com

Private Couple's Intensive

Moving couples from "Shattered to Strong"

Couples that attend Our One-on-One Private Couple's Intensives say it helps them understand and begin or advance the long journey of healing from the immediate and ongoing impacts of porn addiction, sexual addiction, infidelity &/or Intimacy avoidance - for both the Wounding and Wounded partner. We are able to take the time to deep-dive into what's specifically destroying the trust, individually and as a couple, and find the recovery you're desperately trying to either rediscover or discover for the first time.

For many couples, this intensive is their last stop before divorce court or a decision to stay permanent roommates. Couple after couple says that their time at the intensive allowed them to identify and begin the process of healing the hurt and devastation, as well as giving them a new relational system, as their current one just doesn't work for many reasons.

If you choose a Private Couple's Intensive, we will work with you to identify your specific needs to make sure your concerns are fully addressed in a private setting. Our Private Couple's Intensives are 3 days in length and will address both people in the relationship individually as well as the relationship itself.

Like the Guys Group Intensive, our Private Couple's Intensive is a great option for anyone wanting to accelerate the healing process, because intensives take 4-6 months' worth of session work and condense it into 3 days. You will receive an assessment of your unique issues, 7-8 hours per day of instruction, exercises and tools to help you move forward, and a personalized recovery plan for yourself and/or your relationship. We provide you a shame-free environment to address your specific issues.

And, if you choose a Private Couple's Intensive, we want you to know that partners are always treated with respect, compassion, and validation for the pain that their partner's issues have caused them. As a partner, you will never be blamed or asked to take any responsibility for your partner's choices. Also, if desired, we have full disclosure and polygraph services available.

Learn more or sign up for a Private Couple's Intensive today
www.BecomingWellInstitute.com

Books and Courses

Moving Couples from Shattered to Strong

REBUILDING TRUST

A Couple's Guide to Healing After Betrayal

MATT BURTON
LAURA BURTON

www.BecomingWellInstitute.com

Books and Courses

Moving Couples from Shattered to Strong

REBUILDING TRUST FOR CHRISTIANS

A Couple's Guide to Healing After Betrayal

MATT BURTON
LAURA BURTON

www.BecomingWellInstitute.com

Books and Courses

Moving Partners from Shattered to Strong

Mending After Betrayal

BOOK AND WORKBOOK

LAURA BURTON

www.BecomingWellInstitute.com

Books and Courses

Moving Partners from Shattered to Strong

Mending After Betrayal

BOOK AND WORKBOOK FOR CHRISTIANS

LAURA BURTON

www.BecomingWellInstitute.com

Books and Courses

www.BecomingWellInstitute.com

Books and Courses

www.BecomingWellInstitute.com

Books and Courses

www.BecomingWellInstitute.com

Books and Courses

www.BecomingWellInstitute.com

Books and Courses

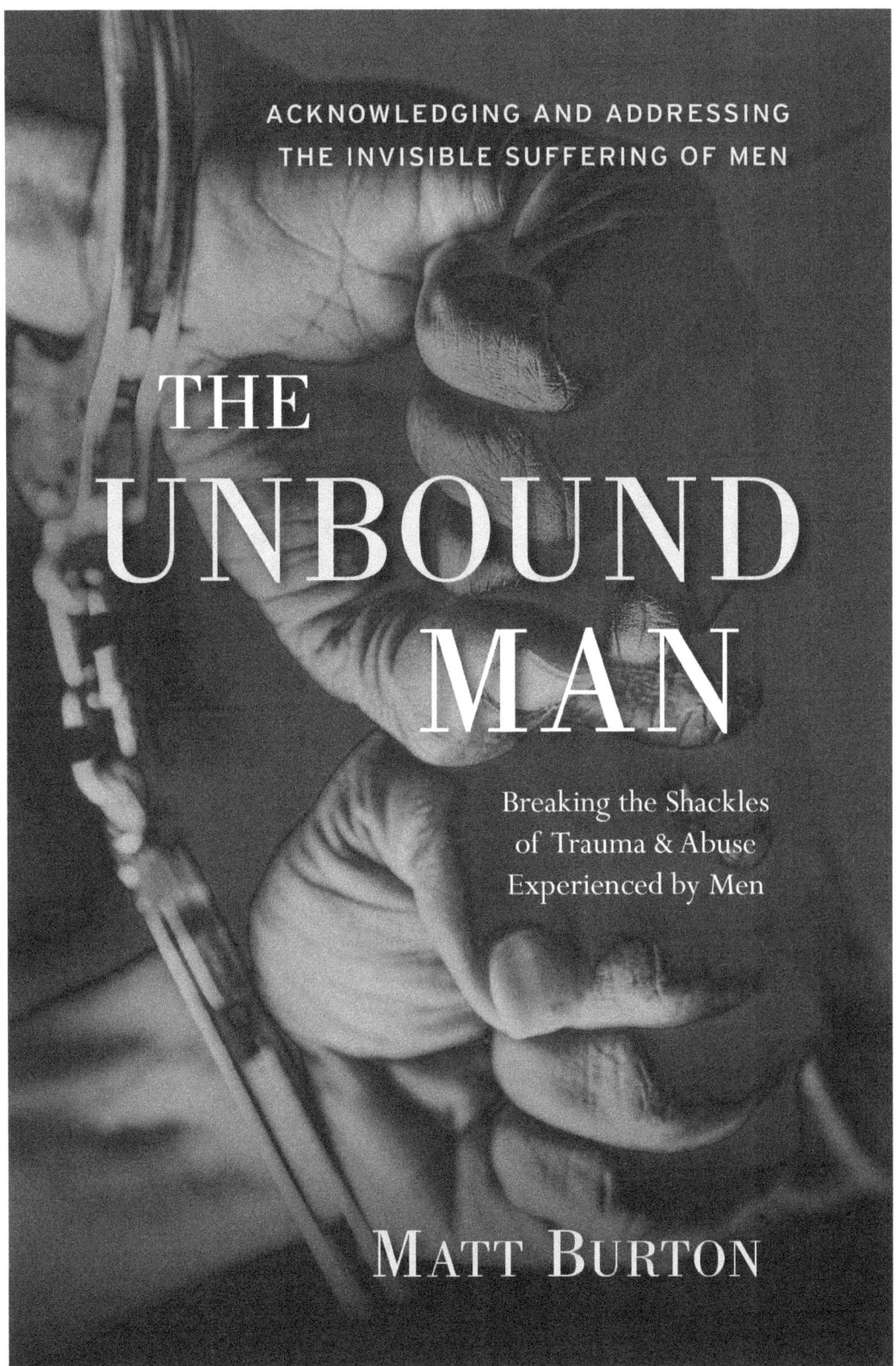

www.BecomingWellInstitute.com

Books and Courses

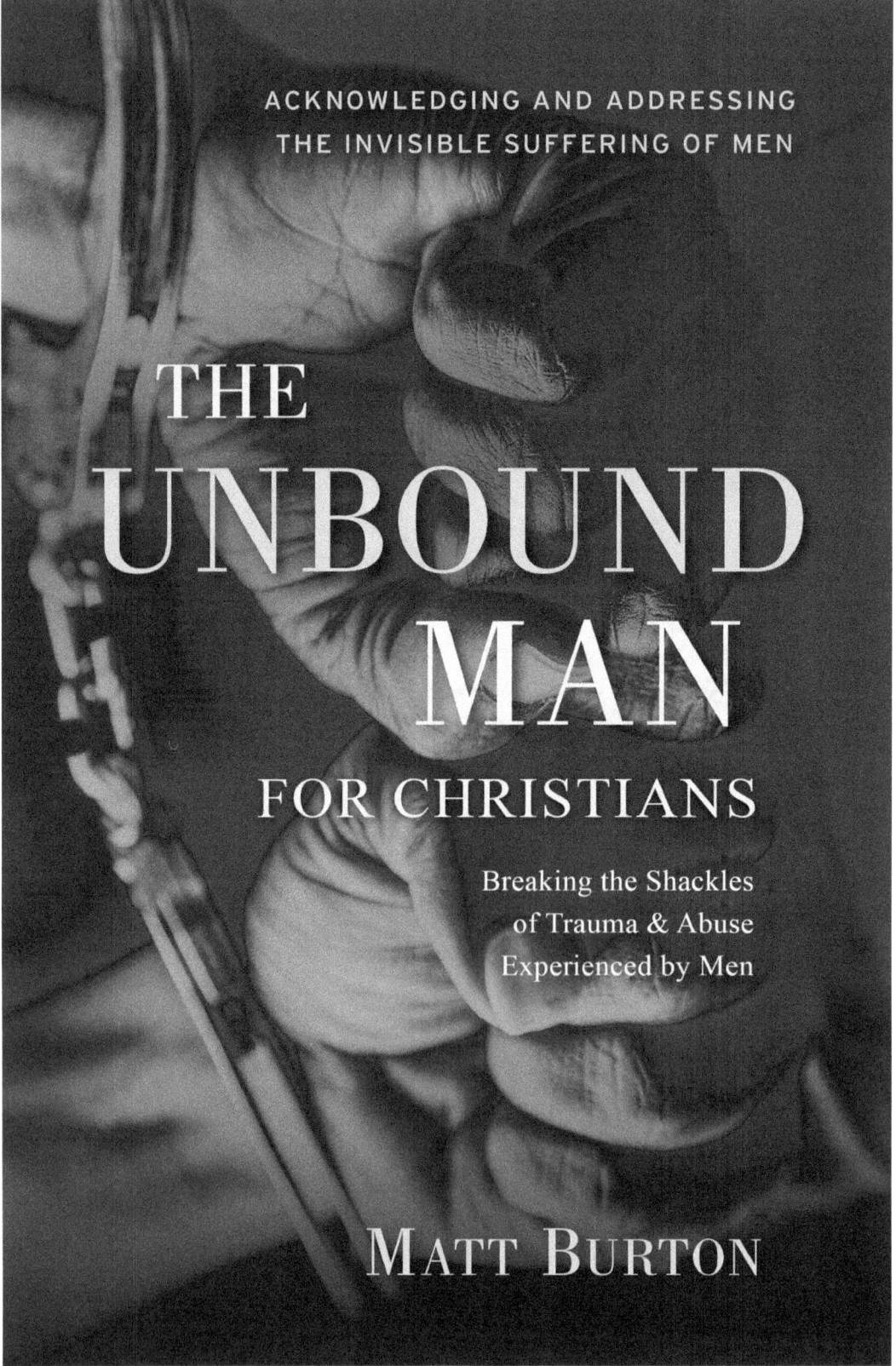

www.BecomingWellInstitute.com

Books and Courses

Books and Courses

Books and Courses

Books and Courses

Connect with Us

 www.facebook.com/mybecomingwell

 Becoming Well (@mybecomingwell)

 Becoming Well (@mybecomingwell)

 www.mybecomingwell.com

 info@mybecomingwell.com

 520-355-5322

www.ingramcontent.com/pod-product-compliance
Lightning Source LLC
LaVergne TN
LVHW081456060526
838201LV00057BA/3058